THE PSYCHOPATH
IN SOCIETY

PERSONALITY AND PSYCHOPATHOLOGY

A Series of Monographs, Texts, and Treatises

David T. Lykken, Editor

1. The Anatomy of Achievement Motivation, *Heinz Heckhausen.* 1966°

2. Cues, Decisions, and Diagnoses: A Systems-Analytic Approach to the Diagnosis of Psychopathology, *Peter E. Nathan.* 1967°

3. Human Adaptation and Its Failures, *Leslie Phillips.* 1968°

4. Schizophrenia: Research and Theory, *William E. Broen, Jr.* 1968°

5. Fears and Phobias, *I. M. Marks.* 1969

6. Language of Emotion, *Joel R. Davitz.* 1969

7. Feelings and Emotions, *Magda Arnold.* 1970

8. Rhythms of Dialogue, *Joseph Jaffe* and *Stanley Feldstein.* 1970

9. Character Structure and Impulsiveness, *David Kipnis.* 1971

10. The Control of Aggression and Violence: Cognitive and Physiological Factors, *Jerome L. Singer* (Ed.). 1971

11. The Attraction Paradigm, *Donn Byrne.* 1971

12. Objective Personality Assessment: Changing Perspectives, *James N. Butcher* (Ed.). 1972

13. Schizophrenia and Genetics, *Irving I. Gottesman* and *James Shields,* 1972°

14. Imagery and Daydream Methods in Psychotherapy and Behavior Modification, *Jerome L. Singer.* 1974

15. Experimental Approaches to Psychopathology, *Mitchell L. Kietzman, Samuel Sutton,* and *Joseph Zubin* (Eds.). 1975

16. Coping and Defending: Processes of Self-Environment Organization, *Norma Haan.* 1977

17. The Scientific Analysis of Personality and Motivation, *R. B. Cattell* and *P. Kline.* 1977

18. The Determinants of Free Will: A Psychological Analysis of Responsible, Adjustive Behavior, *James A. Easterbrook.*

19. The Psychopath in Society, *Robert J. Smith.*

°Titles initiated during the series editorship of Brendan Maher.

THE PSYCHOPATH IN SOCIETY

ROBERT J. SMITH
Department of Psychology
University of Maryland
European Division

ACADEMIC PRESS New York   San Francisco   London   1978
A Subsidiary of Harcourt Brace Jovanovich, Publishers

ACADEMIC PRESS, INC.
111 Fifth Avenue, New York, New York 10003

United Kingdom Edition published by
ACADEMIC PRESS, INC. (LONDON) LTD.
24/28 Oval Road, London NW1 7DX

Library of Congress Cataloging in Publication Data

Smith, Robert Joseph, Date
    The psychopath in society.

    (Personality and psychopathology ;
    Bibliography: p.
    1. Personality, Disorders of--Etiology.   2.   Social
psychiatry.   I. Title.   [DNLM: 1.   Antisocial
personality.   W1 PE861 / WM190 S658p]
RC555.S63   616.8'9   78-7045
ISBN 0-12-652550-1

PRINTED IN THE UNITED STATES OF AMERICA

Contents

2
The Charm and Winning Ways of the Psychopath

3
The Search for a Constitutional Explanation

4
Social Role/Learning Theory Formulations of Psychopathy

5
Cleckley and the Psychopath

6
Psychopathy: Qualitative or Quantitative Entity?

Preface

The literature specifically aimed at psychopathy is surprisingly small, considering the prominence of this diagnosis among mental health professionals, and the legal/moral issues it raises. One estimate of incidence for America alone has been put at 4 million plus (Coleman, 1972), and novelist Norman Mailer thought some years ago (1957) that an estimate of 10 million among the populace might be conservative.

The theorists most concerned with the etiology of this problem have been the psychoanalysts, prominent among them Franz Alexander and Phyllis Greenacre, and psychiatrists like Sheldon Glueck, Hervey Cleckley, and Ben Karpman. Alexander, for example, has given us a developmental rationale stemming from family dynamics in accounting for the "superficiality" of the psychopath. That is, the origins of the adult victim's casual rampages are seen in a failure to develop proper "braking" within the personality. Cleckley—perhaps the most charming to read as well as the most quoted authority—views the psychopath as basically insane: a sad creature who, in spite of frequently superior endowment, inevitably comes-a-cropper because of his failed moral development, dragging those who have trusted him down into the abyss of his own inevitable denouement.

At a more descriptive level we have had the elaborate classifications proposed by continental theorists. These have usually been formulated on the basis of constitutional, hereditary factors (cf. Schneider, 1940; Henderson, 1939; Kretschmer, 1940).

But there are other ways to view the psychopath, and it is my purpose to subject them to scrutiny here, while suggesting, I hope, some relatively novel projections as well. For example, there is an accelerating effort to put this problem on an experimental basis through the work of such researchers as Eysenck, Quay, and Hare. But these people seem rarely to be talking to one another, let alone to the psychoanalysts or social-role theorists such as Gough. The latter inadvertently brings the issue of role playing and its relation to behavioristic analyses in general sharply to the fore in his attempts to ground the nature of psychopathy in inadequate role playing, opening a veritable Pandora's Box of definitional problems in the process. Unfortunate too is the confusion created when young delinquents, whose acting out may mask the entire range of psychiatric disorders, are routinely labeled psychopaths. To put it mildly, research on the psychopath has been seriously confounded by such casual labeling.

It is precisely because the psychopath so defies our traditional mental (un)health categories—yet persists and even grows as a problem for society—that his existence creates such a challenge for the theorist and diagnostician. I propose here to look at Western culture at large in an effort to shed light on this phenomenon. Thus even a casual observer of capitalistic systems can see that the psychopath possesses many of just those traits, behaviors if you like, which augur successful negotiation of the thickets of the marketplace. Yet textbooks and theorists (e.g., Buss, 1966; Cleckley, 1976; Page, 1971; Schneider, 1950; Ullmann and Krasner, 1969) typically ignore such pressures, or gloss over them. The environment for most theorists appears to stop with the immediate family.

Because of "encouragement from without," i.e., the marketplace, it may be argued that psychopathy can be much more fruitfully looked on as the logical extreme, or the fantastic exaggeration perhaps, of what our Western societies not only tolerate, but virtually demand of us if we want to win fame and fortune. This view represents a sharp departure from the traditional one-sided psychiatric–psychoanalytic picture of the psychopath as an anomaly who has not been appropriately socialized, or who is constitutionally immoral. Part of my purpose here, then, is precisely to present this antidote.

What may prove extremely important to the future incidence of psychopathy in Western culture, most especially the American, is the tendency of the counterculture to renounce just those values which most authorities agree are part-and-parcel of the psychopath's bag-oftricks, and which permit him to manipulate those who share these values: pursuit of possessions, social recognition, worship of the conventionally attractive, for example.

Whether such a cultural motif, even if slowly ascendent, could replace the reigning materialism; whether indeed it could itself resist being exploited by being converted into that very motif rejected—witness the modishness of simple jeans and what they have come to cost à la mode—is a question to be remarked and followed rather than answered in the present. Some researchers, for example Argyris (1969; 1975), are optimistic about the potential for such changes.

A clue to an answer regarding the inevitability of psychopathic-like behaviors may lie in the incidence of such behaviors in cultures or subcultures which project quite other values than those of the marketplace. For example, cultures or subcultures reflecting cooperative, group-oriented philosophies in preference to a competitive, individualistic motif. To this end it is instructive to examine what theory and statistics are available from eastern lands, for example, and in general to address psychopathy from the point of view of quite different social systems. Still the problems of definition, differential diagnosis, and statistical and reporting idiosyncrasies render any question of direct cultural comparisons moot, even though it is perhaps valuable to collect in one place—as a starting point—those figures available.

It is my intent and hope that this book will not only bring a fresh perspective to the study of psychopathy—and thereby be of interest to the professional mental health worker and theorist—but also be of sufficient timeliness and interest to engage a lay reader as well. The way from, e.g., Norman Mailer's *The White Negro* (1957) to Eysenck's (1964) speculations on cortical differences between neurotics and psychopaths is long, but they are after all concerned with the same basic syndrome, and I see no reason why they should not share one book cover.

To the best of my knowledge the full range of approaches to the psychopath—from cross-cultural, physiological, and behavioral perspectives—has not yet been brought under one cover for comparative consideration. In doing this, I do not pretend to be able to give exhaustive attention to each and every of these approaches. Rather I aim to point out the basic strengths and weaknesses of each strategy and relate them to my major perspective. To this end I present the ensuing pages.

1

The Evolving Definition of the Psychopath: An Example of the Sociology of Science

The history of the labeling of the behaviors traditionally designated psychopathy presents in microcosm a social history of attitudes toward abnormal states in general. Indeed it is necessary to look at concepts of abnormality historically in order to find the key to varying views of psychopathy. Because psychopathy has never really yielded to specific organic or genetic elements, the criteria for imputing the diagnosis are especially murky, and socioethical factors as cause agents have been permitted the widest leverage. One can look at the changing labels earned by the psychopath as a brief lesson in the sociology of abnormal psychology.[1] The origins that have been ascribed to psychopathic behavior have varied markedly over the approximately two centuries that it has been explicitly recognized. A listing of presumed origins to be subsequently treated includes (a) constitutional weakness, (b) psychodynamic insufficiency, (c) problems-in-living, and (d) inauthenticity —plus variants of these.

Through much of early Western history, the prevailing ideas about

---

[1] By and large I stick doggedly to the designation "psychopath" in what follows, partly for historical reasons, partly for simplicity, and partly from conviction. Occasionally I adopt the designation used by others when discussing an explicit point of view.

the nature of all abnormalities were based on the opinions of the church and its theorists. The power of the church in interpreting the world to the laity in the Middle Ages assured that supernatural elements would play a major part in explaining problem behavior. Therefore the theologians, schooled in such matters, were the logical choice for diagnosing and treating disturbances. Genuinely bizarre behaviors, for example, those which today would be judged psychotic, were thought a response to possession by evil spirits that could be successfully treated by exorcism—by driving out the evil spirit through making the body an unpleasant place to inhabit. The infamous witch hunts of the late Middle Ages with their exquisite tortures grew out of this philosophy. That the torturers derived sexual and aggressive release through this theory is doubtless of no little importance to its lengthy employment.

The psychopath would have escaped this unhappy end because of his ratiocinative powers and good reality contact. It is no surprise, then, that the diagnosis was unknown during the prime era of demon-possession explanations of disturbed behavior. There were people who acted out in manipulative and egocentric fashion, but labels other than abnormality would have been affixed to them.[2] The formal recognition of psychopathy had to await more socially complex times: times during which the conditions and nature of existence were more in flux than those current in the rigid class structures and hence restricted behaviors of Europe of the Middle Ages.

PINEL AND SOCIAL REVOLUTION:
MORAL IMBECILITY

Under the rigid caste structure of prerevolutionary France, one can hardly imagine a liberalized view of abnormality emerging. From about the twelfth century, gradual inroads were made in the absolute liability of the trespasser for his deeds. But the main criterion for ascertaining sanity remained strict and was based on the Old Testament of the Bible: One must have been either a child or judged an idiot (Platt & Diamond, 1965) to escape culpability.

The French Revolution of 1789 was a moral revolution in concept—

[2]Rotenberg and Diamond have likened the "rebellious son" of the Old Testament to the psychopath. The former was defined as "an 'evil one' who should be executed; this penalty was prescribed if both of the following two elements were present: (1) rebelliousness despite admonishment and (2) drunkenness and gluttony (later associated with stealing) [1971, p. 37]." Executions were rare, but the rebellious son was not exempted from criminal responsibility.

even if this may have been corrupted in practice—and was instrumental in providing the soil from which so-called moral therapy was permitted to flower. Paris at this time was pulsing with "liberty, equality, fraternity." This revolution against the divine rights of birth, which was to alter the social structure of the entire Western world, was also essential ground for overthrowing the prevailing view of mental problems as demon possession. The deviate of the Middle Ages had been typically seen as a hopeless outcast cursed by the gods and by man. But it was Phillipe Pinel's century, as Zilboorg has said, "which proclaimed the importance of the inalienable rights of man [Zilboorg & Henry, 1941, p. 280]." Pinel's dramatic successes at the Bicêtre and other French institutions, through the employment of compassion and gentle treatment, stemmed no doubt in part from his conviction about what effect such treatment would have on persons cruelly locked away. He noted what treatment was customarily like in his day and how it would change in his hands:

> Public mental asylums have been considered places of confinement and isolation for dangerous patients and pariahs. Therefore their custodians, who in most cases are inhuman and unenlightened, have taken the liberty of treating these mentally sick in a most despotic, cruel, and violent manner, though experience continually shows the happy results of a conciliating attitude, of a kind and compassionate firmness. Empiricism has often profited from this realization due to the establishing of asylums suitable for mental patients; numerous cures were discovered, but no substantial literary contributions to the progress of science were made. On the other hand, the blind routine of a great number of medical men has moved always within the narrow circle of numerous bloodlettings, cold baths, and violent and repeated showers, with almost no attention paid to the *moral side of the treatment*. Thus in all aspects of the subject man has neglected the purely philosophical viewpoint of the derangement, the exact history of the precursory symptoms, the course and end of the attack if it is an intermittent one, the rules of interior policy in the hospitals, the careful definition of those circumstances which make certain remedies necessary and those which make them superfluous. For in this illness as in many others the skill of the physician consists less in the repeated use of remedies than in the careful art of using them or avoiding them at the right moment [quoted in Zilboorg & Henry, 1941, p. 337].

Recognition of psychopathy as a specific disorder is typically dated to Pinel, who was appointed to the Bicêtre in Paris in 1792, early in the postrevolutionary humanitarian period. He ascribed the label *emportement maniaque sans delier* in 1801 to a man of wealthy and aristocratic heritage who was given to savage and seemingly unprovoked aggressiveness, in spite of his enviable social position. However, according to Pinel, "when unmoved by passion" he showed good judgment and capable management of his affairs. After pushing a woman who had verbally attacked him into a well, killing her, he was confined to the Bicêtre (Rotenberg & Diamond, 1971).

Pinel's passionate espousal of appropriate treatment for those unfortunates locked away and cruelly treated is itself intensely moral and commanded that the hospital environment must change. It is no wonder then that a person like the angry aristocrat, who had all the social and environmental advantages and nonetheless behaved so strangely, could be judged mad, for he had not the grounds for his abnormal behavior of these lesser, more socially maligned inmates. It was not difficult, therefore, to judge him a victim of some sort of moral character defect.

The American Response to Pinel

It is surely no accident that the leading psychiatrist in America, Benjamin Rush, a contemporary of Pinel's and a signer of the revolutionary Declaration of Independence, could also view insanity as moral derangement. America, with its strong religious ethic and egalitarian creed, was readily susceptible to viewing mental illness as a failure of the right moral–social climate. Rush, however, assumed that the moral faculty was primarily congenital, and if defective and coupled with good intelligence, resulted in psychopathic cases. As Noel and Carlson point out, while Rush's belief about the innate nature of morality may have violated the strict associationism common to empiricism, his view "rescued morality from stark mechanical hedonism [1973, p. 373]." This view may have pleased the Puritan Fathers, with their firm faith in God, but the writings of Locke, Hume, Bentham, and Mill then provided the philosophic underpinning for the American faith in a democratic environment as basic to the good society.

By the middle of the nineteenth century in America, Pinel's philosophy of treatment, framed in an increasingly influential environmentalism, was quite well entrenched. The prevailing view was that morality in the individual and an unsympathetic environment were the basic causes of abnormality, and the helping institution would have to overcome these effects. Stockton (California) State Hospital superintendent Shurtleff's statement of 1867, is one that many Americans would probably still agree with 100 years later:

> Fast living, intemperance, disastrous speculations, sudden reverses of fortune, disappointments, separation from family and friends, and an unsettled condition of life, are causes of mental derangement which exist more or less in all civilized countries, but which are supposed to be specially prevalent and influential in California [quoted in Savino & Mills, 1967].

The ideas of liberty and equality were a basic part of the ethos of the founding of the American republic just as with the French, and the sense of moral righteousness accompanying the successful struggle for independence encouraged the belief that those who deviated might have problems of "will" or "warped morality." Pritchard (1835) provided a widely influential formulation of psychopathy viewed as moral insanity:

> There is a form of mental derangement in which the intellectual functions appear to have sustained little or no injury, while the disorder is manifested principally or alone in the state of the feelings, temper or habits. In cases of this nature the moral or active principles of the mind are strongly perverted or depraved; the power of self-government is lost or greatly impaired and the individual is found to be incapable, not of talking or reasoning upon any subject proposed to him but of conducting himself with decency and propriety in the business of life [quoted in Preu, 1944, p. 923].

Rather than being abnormal because of constitution or "birthright," an oppressive environment could be a decisive factor in such behaviors. Mental disorder was hence curable and Pinel's prescription of good works in a nurturant environment was the treatment of choice. So-called "moral therapy" became common in the eastern United States not long after the turn of the nineteenth century and reached its height in America in mid-century: The life it experienced was intense but short.

EARLY LEGAL DEFINITIONS OF INSANITY AND SOCIAL REFORM

In spite of fundamentally dissimilar missions, the fields of law and abnormal psychology have had a mutual influence upon one another with regard to the theory and handling of deviance. Dreher has summarized well the traditional antagonism inherent between the law and psychological views of abnormality. He noted that criminal law is committed to the theory that individuals have free choice and thus moral responsibility, whereas the behavioral sciences generally assume that human acts are determined by physical facts, using "physical" in the broadest sense. Also, behavioral scientists are "patient-treatment" oriented, while the law is oriented toward "social orderliness" (1967, p. 47). The stubborn issues of determinism and responsibility are particularly relevant to psychopathy, especially as they impinge on morality before the law. The psychopath appears behaviorally as responsible for his actions as any other "normal" criminal offender.

In many respects "legal enlightenment" both preceded Pinel's "moral enlightenment" and carried on substantially beyond the period. As early as the thirteenth century the English judge Bracton was central to bringing church ideas on morality and legal tenets of social responsibility together under one judgment process. Bracton was active in the King's Court as well as ecclesiastically, and was well placed to see the virtues and benefits of each aspect: secular liability and church morality. He is credited with forwarding the recognition of moral guilt in questions of legal responsibility at least to the extent that children and those considered idiots or mad were not judged culpable (Quen, 1974).

But this was a long way and a long time from being able to excuse a healthy "rational" adult from crime because of moral failing. Such cases were still largely thought to be failures of will and/or some blend of religious failing and character inadequacy. Change was slow in coming, because questions of morality were at the very root of ideas concerning man's nature and changing interpretations represented a challenge to powerful vested authorities. How free is the Will is a question which has plagued the definition and prosecution of psychopathy, and is a continuing topic for heated debate.

According to Dreher (1967) the English case of *Rex* v. *Arnold* in 1724 permitted establishing proof of insanity as an exemption from intent, without however, specifying the nature of that insanity: the so-called "wild beast test" (Platt & Diamond, 1965). Thus the insanity had to be "total" in order to permit the judgment that the accused was unable to form the criminal intent. "Total" here seems to have meant mad in the raving psychotic sense. Because he showed "vestiges of rationality" in spite of clear signs of disturbance, e.g., he could figure, bargain, and make purchases, defendant Edward Arnold, who had shot and wounded English Lord Onslow, was found guilty (Quen, 1974).

The M'Naghten case of 1843 established a new milestone of legal liberality regarding culpability: Responsibility could not be charged when the accused can be shown to have his reason so impaired that he is unaware of the nature and quality of his act. Daniel M'Naghten was "a paranoid Glasgow woodturner" (Quen, 1974) who shot Edward Drummond, the private secretary to Robert Peel, thinking it was the English Prime Minister himself, because he was told what to do by "the voice of God." A clarifying clause to M'Naghten emphasizes how far the legal profession in England—which influenced standards in many lands—had moved from the early criterion of strict culpability: M'Naghten was acquitted because he did not "know the nature and quality of the act that he was doing or . . . he did not know he was doing what was wrong." The M'Naghten decision appears not to go far enough to excuse the psychopath, since *to know* emphasizes cognitive functions and is likely to be interpreted as knowing what is right or wrong in the legal rather than the moral sense. With this criterion the psychopathic personality would remain responsible for his behavior, since he is not considered even by his most liberal defenders of today to be unaware that, e.g., killing another is wrong.

A RETURN TO FATALISM: CONSTITUTIONAL PSYCHOPATHIC INFERIORITY

There were powerful counterforces afoot in the mid-nineteenth century which bode ill for the "Pinel movement" both abroad and in America. One potent element was the increasing success of organic medicine in tracing the roots of illness. For example, as early as 1857 Esmarsch and Nessen suggested that the mental disorder general paresis might be caused by syphilitic infection. The later substantiation of this hypothesis by Noguchi and Moore in 1913, through isolation of the syphilis spirochete in the brain of a paretic patient, gave great impetus to the search for an organic basis for other forms of mental disturbance. Furthermore physical causation was judged to be far easier to treat than nebulous "moral causes" (Savino & Mills, 1967). Biochemical researchers today maintain the conviction that the discovery of an organic cause for mental disturbances will render them easier to treat.

Related to the concept of an organic basis for mental disorders is the view that some members of a group are naturally inferior to others. The triumph of Darwinian evolutionary theory in the sciences contributed heavily to this position. The importance of Darwin's theory regarding treatment of deviance lay in its suggestion that some representatives of the species would be less fit by virtue of free selection in mating, and that atavistic mutants were to be expected in the thrust for species survival. The studies of the Jukes and Kallikak families seemed to support the tenet that bad seeds lead to unfit offspring. While the idea that moral failure of the psychopath was due to some sort of inherent weakness had been voiced earlier in the century, it was not until 1888 that Koch introduced the term "psychopathic inferiority" in Germany and attributed it to hereditarily determined weakness. Preu's discussion suggests how well the idea had taken hold:

> Since Koch (1891)[3] introduced the term "psychopathic inferiority" the tendency has been to conceive of the basic difficulty as genetically determined and to place the group designated as psychopathic in the class of congenital defect states together with the intellectually defective or feebleminded [Preu, 1944, p. 927].

Koch's term replaced the earlier "moral insanity," and found acceptance both in Europe and America. According to Guttmacher (1953)

[3]The earlier date appears to be the correct one.

it was Adolph Meyer, having earlier left Germany for America, who in 1905 added "constitutional" to Koch's designation of inferiority. Kurt Schneider and Eugen Bleuler are examples of prominent continental theorists who view psychopathic behavior as emotional and moral deviation based on constitutional factors (Kallwas, 1969).

The rise of what might be called the "biogenetic model" did much to undermine moral therapy in America after a short, if relatively success-ful, life (Bockhoven, 1963). While encouraging a rate of patient discharge hitherto unknown in mental health circles, sociopolitical factors, such as facility overcrowding and the social application of Darwin's ideas, struck the mortal blow. The previously mentioned Stockton State Hos-pital, a bastion of moral therapy, opened with 150 patients and by 1869 had 920—more than triple the 250 recommended by moral therapists (Savino & Mills, 1967). An important emphasis of moral therapy was the personal contact of staff and patient, and this necessitated small re-habilitative units.

A major factor in this herding of patients into larger and larger institutions seems to have been the heavy tide of destitute immigrants to America toward the close of the nineteenth century. Immigrants have rarely been well off socially or financially, but these were truly the downtrodden of their native lands, lured by America's promise: Greeks, Italians, Eastern Europeans. Language and cultural differences between these immigrants and the preindustrial era English and Scotch-Irish already at home in America created an additional barrier to adjustment. The exploitation of these poorly assimilated immigrants in the early industrial sweat shops of the eastern United States is a well-known phenomenon needing no special documentation here. Bockho-ven has argued that even Dorothea Dix, whom he believes must have known the value of moral treatment and was the most successful single lobbyist in United States legislative history, failed to take action on the issue of holding down hospital size to manageable proportions. In his opinion, she did not find the pauper immigrants worthy of this effort (Bockhoven, 1965, p. 385). As patients, these persons came inevitably on the rolls of the publicly supported institutions where they tended to remain, swelling inmate populations to huge proportions. State and county hospitals, virtually from the necessity of their size, returned to the segregation and caretaker role from which moral therapy had of-fered a brief, enlightened respite.

Other factors contributing to patient build-up were the seemingly inevitable decline in success that treatment techniques experience (see the current community mental health situation as example), and the accumulation of patients probably suffering clear organic brain syndromes (Savino & Mills, 1967) who were more or less refractory to any environmental changes. In his report to the California state legislature in 1902, Superintendent Clark concluded:

> The principle primary cause of insanity is the same in California as elsewhere, neither more mysterious nor more potent, it dates far back, it is persistent, it is cumulative. Of course I can only refer to heredity [Savino & Mills, 1967, p. 368].

In sum, the prominent forces in America ensuring pessimism regarding the prospects for a deviant were primarily three: (*a*) the influx of immigrants who were poor and socially maladapted; (*b*) the decline of moral therapy in favor of biological determinism leading to custodial separation; (*c*) Darwin's work receiving full social attention through protagonists such as Thomas Huxley, and the research of Sir Francis Galton.

Darwin's theory was the most important of these factors. By the time of Galton's work and Koch's new definition, Darwin's ideas were widely accepted by both medical and nonmedical science. Thus, while social–moral treatment may have been thought right for some who could profit from it, what should be done with those who were inherently stupid or inadequate and furthermore lacked a sense of proper American morality? Better simply to keep them from polluting the main social stream. The history of the first half of the twentieth century is one of locking patients away in increasingly large and impersonal mental hospital complexes. Diagnoses stressing the incorrigibility of deviation corresponded to the hopeless situation in which the bulk of mental hospital inmates were to be found.

THE FREUDIAN ERA:
THE PSYCHOPATH AS MENTALLY ILL

The period of full awakening to Freudian psychodynamic theory in America dates roughly from the 1920s. Freud delivered his famous Clark lectures in Worcester, Massachusetts in 1912. The rise of Freud's structural model of mental life permitted encompassing behavior judged antisocial within the framework of inadequate superego formation. The sufferer has failed to introject the requisite moral prerogatives. While the superego comes in from outside, it is an internal mechanism and, at least in traditional theory, once formed as a residue of the oedipal triangle, remains relatively impervious to social storms around it. There is, then, in this view of moral deviance, a failure in the personality structure. Grounds for inadequate formation of the

superego have been attributed to various "family triangles." Examples
are

1. For the middle class psychopath—a successful, distant, authorita-
   rian father with a frivolous, indulgent (read highly feminized),
   seductive mother. The parents are self-centered and, rather than
   being affectionate, indulge the child to the extent that he or she
   mistakes appearance for feelings and becomes charming and manipulative (Buss on Greenacre, 1966).
2. For the "destructive psychopath"—a rejecting mother leads to a
   hostile and rejective male child who vents hostility on all who pass
   his way.
3. For the impersonator—his lack of identity stems from seeming
   failure to achieve identification with a potential variety of mother
   types including apathetic, indulgent, or multiple mothers, e.g., as
   might frequently occur with a child in an institution (Buss on
   Frankenstein, 1966).

The true psychopath then is not constitutionally inferior, but psycho-
dynamically inferior. Buss (1966) put this in sharp relief:

> psychopathy (irresponsible, amoral behavior), alcoholism and sexual deviance. They
> all share the same criterion of abnormality, bizarreness [p. 430]. . . . Psychopathy is
> exceptional in that the personality features themselves are abnormal. For example,
> some normal individuals lack warmth and feeling for their fellow beings, but the
> psychopath is alone in his tendency to treat others as objects rather than as fellow
> beings [p. 431].

Psychoanalysts have had little luck with treating these cases. Perhaps
this is because analysis traditionally has aimed at loosening an overly
strict superego, whereas it is precisely the psychopath's lack of inhibition that highlights his behavior. The lack of potential for love and basic
trust in these cases, as they are judged by many analysts, makes forming a meaningful therapeutic relation extremely difficult. Furthermore
psychopaths rarely come voluntarily for treatment and so beginning
motivation to change is a serious problem.

In the preceding examples the nuclear family takes the blame for
providing inadequate models for the child, primarily because of inadequate and superficial feelings among the parents for the offspring.
Examples are usually confined to the male child, and mother is the focus
of inadequacy for failing to inculcate genuine empathic humanness in
her boy. Society in the larger, cultural sense is given little notice as a
factor in these superficial interpersonal relationships. Cleckley discusses perhaps the most extreme view in this direction, attributing it to

the psychoanalyst Adelaide Johnson. In her example of a truly "sick" family, the parents are credited with criminal impulses and unconsciously project them on the offspring, who actualizes the wishes through irresponsible, immoral behavior, providing the parents vicarious satisfaction (Cleckley, 1968). This is a novel, tantalizing formulation which seems, however, difficult to test—unconscious criminal impulses lend no easy identification.

This era of placing culpability with the parents is still very much with us, although it probably reached its zenith in the 1940s and 1950s. These were the years during which it was fashionable to blame the psychodynamics of the nuclear family for all quirks—psychotic, neurotic, or criminal—that appeared in the young. In the 1970s the shift has been to look at the family as forming a dynamic unit, but the conjugal family still earns top billing as the pot in which pathological behaviors are brewed.

THE COURTSHIP OF PSYCHIATRY AND THE LAW: SICKNESS IN THE COURTROOM

> If treatment failed, Duker should not have been returned to society. Yet he "served his sentence" and, under present law, he had to be released. Legal recognition of Duker's mental abnormality and "irresponsibility" would not have been "softness"; it would have been a realistic, necessary step in the protection of society [McCord & McCord, 1964, p. 177].

This somber judgment of the McCords referring to a "murderous psychopath" indicates the power gained by the "mental illness" model of deviance since the conquest of the mental health field in America by Freudian theory. Psychopaths are seen as ill and needing to be retained for treatment. This "abnormal irresponsibility" mentioned by the McCords represents a return to the nineteenth century position that the moral sense could become more or less independently diseased. When law as an expression of society swung around behind the medical interpretation of psychopathic criminality, it meant not only that psychiatry would become a power as a "friend of the court," but that it would also have the major voice in determining treatment in such cases.

The gradual, sporadic turning away from individual responsibility toward an illness interpretation of deviation seen in the history of Anglo-Saxon law over the preceding 1000 years has guaranteed the increasing interdependence of law and psychiatry/psychology. The road from absolute Old Testament guilt, where crimes were often settled privately between the families of accuser and accused, to common law where the mental state of the accused could serve to mitigate any action in which he might have engaged, led gradually and inevitably to an encroachment on the law by psychiatric medicine. As indicated, the psychopath stood outside early legal liberalizing changes because of his apparent reasonableness and sanity. Still there are those currently who have taken the position that criminality per se, especially if repetitive, represents "insane behavior." Thus psychopathic persons who come to the attention of the law would be labeled insane because of the "antisocial" element in the diagnosis. It follows readily from this standpoint that anyone committing an act against the law could be confined until he or she shows a "reasonable attitude" and is released from mental institution incarceration. While finally rejecting this reasoning, the McCords (1964) pose an issue which would freeze the blood of many civil liberties advocates:

> Should society, either through legal or private agencies, intervene in the operation of the family? How can such an intrusion take place without violating basic civil liberties? . . . Occasions may well arise, nevertheless, when families producing incipient psychopathic personalities will refuse treatment. Intervention might be advised in such cases as in a case where parents refused to quarantine their child if he suffered from measles [McCord & McCord, 1964, p. 193].

In spite of this broadside aimed specifically at psychopaths, they have been less affected in recent history by "liberalizing" strategies than schizophrenic or brain-damaged persons held for treatment. A psychopath can usually demonstrate rationality or "correct attitude" on demand and obtain release from those who would force his commitment. Modern institutions provide him, indeed, with a haven from police pursuit and an environment within which his manipulative skills show themselves to best advantage. Bureaucracies are nurturant psychopathic environments—at both the administrative and service ends.

The analogy of psychopathy with measles or similar organic illnesses fails on numerous counts, not least against the argument that holds psychopathy as having cultural determinants. However, medically based commitments have come relatively late in the history of legal practice; things have not always been so good for the psychopath. In 1881 when Guiteau shot President James Garfield, his defense focused on the idea that he was morally insane, after M'Naghten, and therefore not responsible for the murder. The prosecution countered with psychiatrists who maintained that he could tell right from wrong. A U.S. President seems the wrong individual to assassinate even in a changing professional climate about the nature of madness, and Guiteau was convicted and executed.

In *Parsons* v. *The State of Alabama* (1887), the consideration of volition in criminal behavior was added to the M'Naghten knowledge-of-right-or-wrong criterion of culpability. This case represented another major step in the direction of liberalized accountability for trespassing on the law. It was ruled that responsibility should be abrogated not only if the defendant were unable to make a cognitive distinction regarding right versus wrong, but also if, granting that facility, the accused was nonetheless unable to choose between the two. This became known as the "irresistible impulse test" (Dreher, 1967). This opened wide Pandora's box and brought the law to uncomfortable dependence on expert medical opinion. Under Parsons there is simply no possibility of an objective criterion of guilt. What does it mean to have an irresistible impulse and how is that to be determined? Under this criterion the psychopath would present a strong case for innocence because one of the major diagnostic signs of psychopathy is the inability to refrain from exercising his or her momentary whim.

In the twentieth century various modifications have been offered to Parsons in an attempt to clarify the distinction between what is a resistible and an irresistible impulse. In *Durham* v. *The United States,* the court of appeals of the District of Columbia (1954) concurred in putting decisions about criminal responsibility and mental disease in the hands of the mental health experts. Monte Durham had had a history of bad check passing, unfitness for military service and petty theft, as well as confusion and seeming hallucinations which earned him various psychiatric labels including that of psychopath, both with and without psychosis. However most expert witnesses could not classify him as "insane on the basis of not knowing right from wrong," à la M'Naghten, although they judged him to be mentally abnormal. Durham was subsequently imprisoned. Judge Bazelon, in then reversing the lower court decision, enunciated the principle that if a criminal act was the product of mental disease or defect, culpability could not be charged. His hope was to relieve the court of deciding the rationality of the defendant. This represented a further step in bringing the mental health expert into courtroom judgments. The begged question of the nature of mental disease, with its ramifications for the criminal act, naturally calls out the psychiatrist or psychologist. The psychopath again presents an ambiguous figure, since by the usual criteria of mental derangement he "passes" the test of normality.

The *United States* v. *Currens* case (1961) added to the Durham criterion of mental disease or defect the criterion of *substantial incapacity to conform to the law* on the part of the defendant at the time of committing the act. "Substantial incapacity to conform" is grossly vague, and perhaps because of its very vagueness served—much as the Parsons decision to M'Naghten—to open the way for exoneration of psychopathic behavior, not otherwise able to be characterized as insane or mentally incapacitated.[4] It is generally accepted in the definition of the psychopath that moral failing and absence of guilt feelings are key aspects of the syndrome. This evolution in the law toward exempting from criminal responsibility those who are judged incapable of experiencing right or wrong because of insanity or impulsiveness brings the psychopath directly to the gates of legal decision as a test case. The psychopath is often clever and seemingly rational, frequently manipulating on the fringe of the law, and often seemingly incorrigible despite his or her protestations to reform. Is this person sane or insane?

The successive legal decisions softening the path for legal responsibility have not been applied in a uniform direction. According to Dreher, as late as 1967, 39 states still hewed to M'Naghten, 14 followed Parsons' irresistible impulse, with other states spreading their allegiance among other court decisions such as Currens. Still, the thrust of these decisions has been to view and treat the psychopath as a more-than-criminal trespasser whose overall actions must bespeak a mentality on the borderland of sanity. The law, in its obligatory social responsibility, cannot easily go around the knotty sanity question for psychopathy, while psychological theorists, in their rarified environment, can approach the problem in various ways.

BEHAVIORISM AND PROBLEMS IN PSYCHOPATHIC LIVING

> In addition to individual causative factors, consideration should be given to the cultural forces that may contribute to psychopathy. Unfortunately, less research attention has been given to this important area of consideration [McCord & McCord, 1964, p. 87].

This quotation is consistent with the behavioristic model of abnormality, which focuses on behavior as being determined externally, from cultural reinforcements. There is also the emphasis among behaviorists on defining abnormality as the crossing of socio-legal boundaries of the group, of "problems in living" (Szasz, 1960). This "social trespass"

[4]However, Page (1971) reports of the Model Penal Code of the American Law Institute, on which Currens is based: "A second provision of the code, which has not been cited, is designed to exclude as a qualifying mental disease the antisocial conduct of sociopaths [p. 76]." One would wonder how.

criterion suggests that there would be no deviations if there were no specific prohibitions, and runs counter to a model of psychological "sickness" in the individual, against abnormality as a state. According to "social trespass" theory, cultures themselves determine the criteria for judging the rightness of behavior, and behaviorists fondly point to anthropological evidence of wide cultural variability in what is judged normal and abnormal. Still, in adopting behavioral criteria for abnormality, what altered was the focus of judgment, not the evaluation of the behavior itself. The emphasis was now on the behavior not the psyche, but psychopathic behaviors have continued to be seen as malfunctional, inappropriate actions. Consideration of the nature of the society in which the behavior occurs has been just as much ignored as when the focus was on the alienated psyche. Only the label—from psychopath to sociopath—appears to have changed, not the evaluation of the behavior itself.

Preu (1944) noted that as early as 1930 the English psychiatrist G. E. Partridge advocated the term "sociopath" as replacement for psychopath. But rather than calling society to account, the change merely emphasized that the sufferer was out of joint with the group rather than internally perverse. That the designation sociopath seems not to have contributed much to precision in thinking about the psychopath is noted by the McCords, who argue that drunkards, criminals, and sex deviants are pushed into the same class, since they all have social-trespass problems, and differences between such cases are then ignored (1964, p. 20). Their point is well taken when one notes how subjects for research into psychopathy are frequently chosen.

In seeking to explain the persistent problems in living they see among those labeled sociopaths, behaviorists have turned to a study of the conditioning process whereby such maladaptation might have come to exist. A typical design is to contrast the acquisition of a galvanic skin response (GSR) to a mild punishment stimulus such as electric shock to the finger, administered for an erroneous response. Usually contrasted groups of socially delinquent subjects and normal controls are used. Since psychopaths are typically diagnosed as being low in anxiety, the prediction is that conditioned responses should be more difficult to induce in such persons because a minimum of anxiety is judged necessary to facilitate learning the response. Numerous studies (cf. Eysenck, 1964; Hare, 1970; Lykken, 1957) have found this to be the case. This finding is commonly extended to the larger social context. It is argued that the psychopath is not able fully to profit from punishment because he hasn't the normal anxiety in anticipating the outcome of his antisocial actions, and hence exercises his whim without inhibition. The analogy is indeed a neat one, although, given the artificiality of the experimental setting, one may wonder how seriously the psychopath would take a shock-to-the-finger situation, and thus how accurately it depicts his response to his culture. The psychopath might look on this as a game, e.g., a challenge to withstand. There has been, as far as this writer has observed, no suggestion by behaviorists that the culture may itself offer an ambiguous model as reinforcer, or that the culture may promise little need to be anxious in displaying manipulative behaviors, for example.

Quay's (1965) "stimulation-seeking" hypothesis, also derived from laboratory research, is an interesting biological correlate of the conditioning theory. The assumption is that the psychopath is bored and craves stimulation because of an intrinsically high threshold and more rapid adaptation to stimulation. The hypothesis that those who eventually go beyond even the highly tolerant limits of some societies might be restless, high-energy thrill seekers does not conflict with any theory of the nature of psychopathy. It is at the same time an interesting, testable hypothesis.[5]

Employment of the sociopathy label reached the zenith of its usage in America in the 1950s, which was also the high point of orthodox behaviorism. From the start there were anti- and dyssocial sociopaths (cf. The American Psychiatric Association's *Diagnostic and Statistical Manual,* 1952). They were primarily distinguished in that the latter was the "professional," hardened, if loyal criminal, who would hold to a bond of silence or trust vis-à-vis his comrades-in-arms—a very uncharacteristic psychopathic behavior. It is the writer's impression that outside of America this mafia-like criminality was never seriously regarded as sociopathic, and it has been dropped from the latest edition of the *Diagnostic and Statistical Manual* (APA, DSM-II, 1968). Behaviorists themselves have not always been happy with this latter category. Ullmann and Krasner (1969) observed:

> Including the dyssocial reaction among the current mental illnesses highlights the question of whether criminal behavior is necessarily sick behavior. The dyssocial category, as previously defined, is a label used for individuals with no obvious pathology other than criminal behavior. These people may be excellent fathers and husbands with deep loyalty to their families, friends, and "organizations." Their behavior is not sick, it is illegal [p. 457].[6]

While the term "sick" here is an uncharacteristic departure for avowed behaviorists, the general emphasis on the definition of psy-

[5] It is not undisputed, however; see Guttmacher, 1953; Schachter, 1971.
[6] This and subsequent quotations cited to Ullman and Krasner, 1969 are reprinted by permission of Prentice-Hall, Inc., Englewood Cliffs, New Jersey, from Leonard P. Ullman and Leonard Krasner, *A Psychological Approach to Abnormal Behavior,* © 1969.

chopathy as one who oversteps social limits is close to the main thesis of the writer's position. Ullmann and Krasner sum up:

> it is not conceived that there is an entity called psychopath or sociopath into which an individual can be fitted. It is only possible to describe the behaviors that are disturbing to a society and that therefore receive labels [1969, p. 456].

The first point regarding the legitimacy of the diagnosis is moot, and I shall address it in due course. Suffice it here to say that looking at a syndrome as culturally circumscribed does not commit one necessarily to the phenotypic level of analysis. As to the second I shall attempt to go beyond these authors' limited social view to argue that the morality of those today labeled psychopathic personalities in America are not particularly warped vis-à-vis their society. Because of the tolerance for and even encouragement of psychopathic-like behaviors in and by leading segments of the society, only extreme cases which exceed liberal limits are likely to attain the label psychopath, and then predominantly among the weaker members of the society.

POSTSCRIPT

Since the World Health Organization (WHO) has begun work on systematizing diagnostic classifications world-wide, the term Antisocial Personality (301.7) has been introduced and is gaining currency as the term for designating psychopaths (WHO, 1972). Clearly the literal English meaning of this term carries with it some unfortunate connotations. First, although WHO probably would not want it so (cf. WHO, 1972), "against (anti) society" inevitably brings one to the position of a culturally relative diagnosis. Inasmuch as cultures, at least at the overt level, display startlingly different norms, behaviors transgressing such norms must vary equally startlingly from one to another. This obviously makes cross-cultural discussion of diagnoses based on behaviors alone relatively meaningless. WHO's efforts to arrive at diagnostic agreement among countries would seem to belie stopping at the phenotypic level. Second, there is the point that I will be at pains to make in succeeding chapters: At least in societies which place a premium on competition and material success, the psychopath is not anti-society at all. On the contrary, he is to be seen as the logical and psychological extreme; perhaps as the caricature (Diaz-Guerrero, 1967) who goes beyond the limits—who is extra- not anti-society.

2

The Charm and Winning Ways of the Psychopath

Perhaps the most disarming aspect of the psychopath, a character who is otherwise frequently viewed as an aggressive, murderous law breaker, is his/her display of thoroughly beguiling charm. The periods may be rare in those cases where aggression has gotten the upper hand, but even in the most violent cases earning this label we are shown flashes of winsome charm which appears so natural in the perpetrator that it seems as honest a part of his personality as any of his other distinguishing marks. And it is typically an innocent, even angelic display that gives the observer the feeling that he is in the presence of a lovable, loving pet animal. Indeed I have so rarely read of a case where this guile was missing, that my own inclination is to regard it as basic to the syndrome as is the oft-diagnosed guiltlessness.

Cleckley, who did much with his initial contribution (1941) to bring some order in the English literature to the characterization of this syndrome, lists the following among symptoms of the clinical profile of the psychopath:

1. *Superficial charm and good intelligence*

Alert and friendly in his attitude, he is easy to talk with and seems to have a good many genuine interests. There is nothing at all odd or queer about him, and in every respect he tends to embody the concept of a well-adjusted, happy person. Nor does he, on the other hand, seem to be artificially exerting himself like one who is covering up or who wants to sell you a bill of goods. He would seldom be confused with the professional back-slapper or someone who is trying to ingratiate himself for a concealed purpose. Signs of affectation or excessive affability are not characteristic. He looks like the real thing [1976, p. 338].

2. *Absence of "nervousness" or psychoneurotic manifestations*

Regularly we find in him extraordinary poise rather than jitteriness or worry, a smooth sense of physical well-being instead of uneasy preoccupation with bodily functions. Even under concrete circumstances that would for the ordinary person cause embarrassment, confusion, acute insecurity, or visible agitation, his relative serenity is likely to be noteworthy [1976, p. 340].

3. *Absence of delusions and other signs of irrational thinking*

Not only is the psychopath rational and his thinking free of delusions, but he also appears to react with normal emotions. His ambitions are discussed with what appears to be healthy enthusiasm. His convictions impress even the skeptical observer as firm and binding. He seems to respond with adequate feelings to another's interest in him and, as he discusses his wife, his children, or his parents, he is likely to be judged a man of warm human responses, capable of full devotion and loyalty [1976, p. 339].[1]

Needless to say a person displaying such positive attributes would approach Maslow's "self-actualizing" level or Jung's self realization were it not for the negative qualities which Cleckley and most other clinicians adduce to fill out the psychopathic profile.

That the psychopath should be in one way or another a charmer should surprise no one, for without that quality he would be in no position to manipulate others, whether it is only to win a confidence or to use the other as perhaps a sexual or financial object. An example of this charm and guile is particularly well displayed in the following case, which captures as well as any I know the near innocent charm that attaches to some examples of psychopathy. At the same time it is itself written with charm and wit—but we must not look for psychopathy everywhere! I reproduce the story in its entirety as printed in the *Smith, Kline & French Psychiatric Reporter* (Van Atta, 1965).

I'll Always Remember Arthur

He was a clever thief, an imaginative liar, and one of the handsomest men I have known, with the innocence of a kitten and the morals of a tomcat. His first name was Arthur; his last name doesn't matter. Arthur's IQ bordered on the genius level. Given just one additional gift—good judgment—he could have left his mark in any field of endeavor; lacking it, he became that rarest of human creatures, a completely happy

---

[1] This and subsequent quotations cited to Cleckley, 1976 are reprinted with permission of The C. V. Mosby Co. from Cleckley, H. *The Mask of Sanity,* ed. 5, St. Louis, 1976.

man doing the one thing on earth for which nature had best prepared him. For Arthur, it was being a full-time problem patient in a large state hospital. I worked as an attendant in that hospital 30 years ago. I was Arthur's attendant for more than a year, and he chose me as a special friend, next only to his psychiatrist, Dr. Kiley, in his affections. With Arthur as your friend you did not, as the Hungarians say, need many enemies.

Nonetheless, when the *Reporter* sent me back to the hospital last summer to write about the changing role of attendants, the one person I most wanted to see was Arthur. I learned that he had left the hospital shortly after I did, and under circumstances that were in complete harmony with his past performances.

Arthur was 34 when I first met him, which was the day I was promoted to charge attendant and put in command of one shift on Crane Cottage. All three shifts of attendants on Crane were new and our supervisor had just transferred from another hospital—a situation that Arthur was quick to note. When I reported for duty, he greeted me with outstretched hand, smiling that engaging smile I came to know so well. "Thank God, they've finally sent us an intelligent young man for this ward," he said. "You are new, but you'll learn. Just come to me if you need help." He hesitated, then added, "Dr. Kiley will be giving me a parole of the grounds when he returns from vacation, but we'll both have to work on him, won't we?"

By 3 o'clock, I was wondering how on earth a man of Arthur's intelligence and poise could possibly be a mental patient on a locked ward. The other attendants felt the same, so when the patient in charge of our clothesroom went home, we agreed that Arthur was the logical man to assume this important job—and it *was* important because we were responsible for every stitch of clothing owned by our 80 patients.

A few mornings later Arthur met me wearing a well-cut black suit, a white shirt, two-tone shoes, and a bow tie. Before I could comment, he said, "Thought I'd clean up for a change. One of my girl friends from the city may be out today." Watching him strut up the corridor, I could understand why she might.

Reality struck the moment Dr. Kiley returned. "Oh, no!" he cried, "you shouldn't have put Arthur in that job." A careful inspection of his locker and clothes card showed that Arthur now owned 14 suits, 22 shirts, five pairs of shoes, dozens of new ties, not to mention silk bathrobes, much new underwear, slacks, and sweaters. Each article carried a standard tape from the marking room, stamped with Arthur's name, and there was a roll of unused tapes found in his desk, proving that the patient underground system was efficient. It took a stenographer and two clerks from the administration office almost a month to return the clothes to the proper owners. Arthur looked me straight in the eye, and swore that his many girl friends from the city, out of appreciation for his manhood in previous days, had brought the clothes to him.

When I asked Dr. Kiley to tell me a little more about Arthur, he brought me his case history from the record office. Born into a good farm family in the western part of the state, Arthur had graduated from high school, and had then gone to work for an elderly German farmer who had married a younger woman—she was 52—as his second wife. When the farmer died suddenly at the age of 70, Arthur, then 23, married the widow, who had inherited widow's rights in the valuable farm. Arthur put in one crop, but after silo-filling in the fall went to bed and did not get up again until early the next spring—and then only to attend his wife's funeral. She had been killed in an auto accident on an icy road while coming from town with Arthur's beer. According to the social worker, the widow had been madly in love with her young husband, humoring his every whim, bringing him magazines and books, cooking his special dishes, milking and doing all the chores while Arthur reclined in bed, taking life easy. Children of the previous marriage offered Arthur $500 for the farm—only a fraction of its value—but he accepted it gratefully. He used his small inheritance to go to the city, where he held numerous jobs, but finally drifted down to Skid Row.

Arthur, who had been classified as a "psychopathic personality" by our medical staff, was completely happy at the hospital and often outlined its many benefits to me. "I never had it so good," he said. "I had $200 worth of free dental care last year, free movies, free dances, a free library with good books, and the food is better than the Salvation Army's soup kitchen." The only blight on Arthur's life occurred with the coming of spring, when he would be struck by an uncontrollable cosmic urge. This was always apparent when his stories turned to his past amours, which he would relate in great detail, eyes sparkling as he remembered. At this point his campaign to get back his parole of the grounds became intense, and Dr. Kiley, a truly gentle and understanding man, was almost as vulnerable as his attendants were to Arthur's appeals.

The year before I came to Crane Cottage, Dr. Kiley had granted Arthur freedom of the grounds and had assigned him to the farm detail to work in the vegetable fields. Directly across from the hospital's farmlands was a fine private farm, with a nice house, several barns and silos. Patients went in from the fields at four, but Arthur, with his parole of the grounds, did not have to report back to his ward until nine. He constructed a collapsible roadside stand directly across from this fine farmhouse, where his sign offered fresh vegetables, "picked today," and home-baked bread, "fresh from the oven." People from town, three miles away, were lining up evenings to purchase these superior products from that "nice farmer" on Town Line Road, paying premium prices. The vegetables were off the state farm, the bread was run in relays, as needed, from the patients' bakery by Arthur's assistants. When he had accumulated enough cash for his fling in the city, he took off, ending up with D.T.'s three weeks later. He was taken to the county hospital, then sent back to us.

Arthur was always delighted to get back "home," and the other patients would hang on his words as he told them in great detail of his conquests in the city, some of them probably true.

As May approached during my year on Crane Cottage, Arthur's cosmic urge became full-blown, and I could see Dr. Kiley weakening. After he finally gave in and assigned Arthur to work in the plumbing shop, giving him a parole of the grounds, he told me, a little sheepishly, that he didn't expect any reformation in Arthur's character. Then added, grinning, "But everyone ought to have the benefit of a second chance."

Five weeks after going on the plumbing gang, Arthur took off for the city. The source of his vacation money became known when the big packing company near the hospital reported that one of our patients had dismantled the copper plumbing of its little soap factory which was used only in the fall when hams were being processed. Unfortunately, Arthur had used a hacksaw rather than a pipe wrench to dismantle the long pipes before hauling them to a junk dealer, who had paid him $107 for his "scrap" metal. It cost the state several thousands of dollars to get it reinstalled in the soap factory. Following this, an edict came down from the superintendent: no more freedom of the grounds for Arthur.

I left the wards to become a staff stenographer. Dr. Kiley retired, and one of the young doctors was given his service. One day this young doctor dictated a progress note to me on Arthur. It read: "This patient is highly intelligent, seems to be totally responsible at present, and has asked for an opportunity to work outside. In view of his past record, I have assigned him to work on a detail at the dairy barn, where he will be under the supervision of an employee at all times." He was a kind, trusting young man, and I did not give him my opinion of his decision about Arthur, but I was smiling inwardly as I went to my desk. June was only a few weeks away.

Late in May, a wave of drunkenness broke out among the working patients. The superintendent had just begun an investigation, suspecting employees of selling whiskey to patients, when the great breakthrough erupted one Friday afternoon. Patients were gathering to sing harmony; fist fights broke out in the laundry, at the powerhouse, in the kitchen. More than 30 patients were picked up intoxicated. Several partially emptied gallon cans of a strange smelling and tasting concoction were found with the patients, and it tested 18% alcohol by volume at our lab. Arthur left early that afternoon for the city.

After winning the complete trust of the employee in charge of the dairy barns, Arthur had been given considerable freedom, doing his work well, a veritable model of deportment. However, the many silos connecting to the daily barns were made of wood. Arthur had tapped the silos like sugar maple trees, filling more than a dozen large milk cans with silage juice, to which he added yeast obtained at the bakery. He stored them in an unused bullshed until their contents were ready for marketing. He sold an estimated 100 gallons of the stuff before leaving on his vacation, from which he returned five weeks later, exhausted but happy to be home.

The rest of Arthur's story I learned last summer from a supervisor who had once worked with me as an attendant on Crane Cottage. He said that a doctor had left a copy of a psychiatric journal on his desk, that Arthur had found it and read with special interest a paper describing a new state hospital on the West Coast where a revolutionary approach to treatment was taking place. No locks were used at this hospital; all patients were free to come and go as they pleased; and they had visiting privileges into town. When they worked, they were paid for their services. Arthur had shown this article to my friend, asking him if he believed it. My friend said that it would not be in that medical journal unless it were true. Arthur left his locked ward through a window a few nights later.

The very last communication contained in Arthur's folder was from a state hospital on the West Coast, asking for "any information you might furnish on Arthur _____, who has just entered this hospital as a voluntary patient, and who has admitted previous treatment in your hospital." Perhaps he is still out there. If so, I am sure his attendants and doctors know him well [pp. 8–10].

There seems little necessity of adding to this classic profile of charm and guile. Arthur is an example of one who made use of a system which was good to him; that he over-used it on occasion accounts for his clashes with the authorities. That the nature of his problem was such that he *must* exceed limits can not be discounted. At the same time he seems to have lacked the sustained aggressive ambition which would have permitted him to rise upward in the system—in spite of obvious gifts—where he could ultimately dictate to others.

THE SUPERIOR PSYCHOPATH

In turning to classical literature for expressions of psychopathy, Stone and Stone (1966) present Thomas Mann's famous confidence man, Felix

Krull, a charmer of the first order. In looking back on his youth from the advanced age of 40, Krull says of himself:

> The other boys of the town seemed to me dull and limited indeed, since they ob-
> viously did not share my ability and were consequently ignorant of the secret joys I
> could derive from it by a simple act of will, effortlessly and without any outward
> preparation. They were common fellows, to be sure, with coarse hair and red hands,
> and they would have had trouble persuading themselves that they were princes—and
> very foolish they would have looked, too. Whereas my hair was silken soft, as it
> seldom is in the male sex, and it was fair; like my blue-gray eyes, it provided a
> fascinating contrast to the golden brown of my skin, so that I hovered on the
> borderline between blond and dark and might have been considered either. My
> hands, which I began to take care of early, were distinguished without being too
> narrow, never clammy, but dry and agreeably warm, with well-shaped nails that it
> was a pleasure to see. My voice, even before it changed, had an ingratiating tone and
> could fall so flatteringly upon the ear that I liked more than anything to listen to it
> myself, especially when I was alone and could blissfully engage in long, plausible,
> but quite meaningless conversations with my imaginary adjutant, accompanying
> them with extravagant gestures. Such personal advantages are mostly intangible and
> are recognizable only in their effect; they are, moreover, difficult to put into words,
> even for someone unusually talented. In any case, I could not conceal from myself that I
> was made of superior stuff, or, as people say, of finer clay, and I do not shrink from
> the charge of self-complacency in saying so [quoted in Stone & Stone, 1966, pp.
> 266–267].[2]

While this is Krull describing his own charm, his youthful successes among people leave little doubt that his impact on others was approximately as strong as on himself. Krull was convinced of his being hewn "of finer clay," and the question which this raises about the relation of intelligence and psychopathy is not a new one; as we saw, Cleckley rates it as basic.

A fairly high level of intelligence seems essential to human creativity (McNemar, 1964) and the notion of a creative psychopath has a long and substantial history in the European literature (cf. Frankenstein, 1959; Henderson, 1939; Lange-Eichbaum, 1942), but has received little attention in North America (Cleckley makes oblique reference to the possibility, but does not discuss the considerable literature). Perhaps a reason is that much of the work appears in the German language. Perhaps the accumulating distaste for the idea of intelligence as a trait is involved; some American psychologists have sought to show creativity independent of intelligence (cf. Torrance, 1962).

Or perhaps most importantly the disinclination to see psychopathy among the cultural elite in the United States may also have contributed

---

[2] From "Confessions of Felix Krull, Confidence Man." Reprinted from *Stories of Three Decades* by Thomas Mann. Copyright © 1930, 1936 by Alfred A. Knopf, Inc.

to the lack of discussion of this potential case. If, as the textbooks so often say, National Socialist Hermann Goering was a psychopath, he could certainly qualify as a successful, even creative example. The creative psychopath may be he who grasps the opportunities for exploitation available in a society. In societies where notoriety is basic to success, those who attain the pinnacle of certain fields of endeavor are required to possess a considerable share of those elements of personality that major theorists associate with psychopathy. In America there is an entire industry recently grown up around the "field" of image-building.

Even in those fields where ability must precede image, e.g., professional sport, a large measure of showmanship seems essential to bringing the athlete further in his career. It was often said of Muhammed Ali (Cassius Clay) when he was just another campaigning heavyweight boxer, but given to composing droll poetry, that he was "good for the sport." The reference was not to his boxing skills but to his promotional skills. This facility was remarked repeatedly by "media personalities" and without the irony that might have been expected of some one gratuitously equating sport with show business. Irony was missing because these commentators were absolutely serious: Sport and show business had become for them as one. Such commentators themselves are given to referring to one another as "sports personalities," or "television personalities," as if they derived their Being from the media. This topic of psychopathy and cultural personalities will be treated in some depth later in this essay.

How pathological is the charming and winsome psychopath? Surely it depends on the authority to whom one turns. Cleckley considers them mad; the law, by and large, does not. I should say the majority view does not. I hold with the majority, although it seems to me that there are psychopathic-like behaviors that do have madness at the base of their expression. Such cases can often be distinguished from the psychopath, and I should like now to review some prominent examples.

DISTINGUISHING THE PSEUDOPSYCHOPATH

One of the major difficulties faced by those who would label the psychopath as one who simply has "problems in living" more or less like so many others who come to be called mentally ill (Albee, 1970; Szasz, 1960) is that the acting out style of the psychopath does not distinguish itself readily from certain other syndromes, yet there seem to be meaningful clinical differences. While the distinctions are not simply made, I would not on that account judge them superfluous. Rather the distinctions must be made at a more fundamental level of analysis than the behavioral. This difficult but important task has been pursued by various theorists on the basis of several major diagnostic distinctions. Before addressing those, Cleckley's list of psychopathic symptoms begun earlier is filled out as follows:

1. Unreliability
2. Untruthfulness and insincerity
3. Lack of remorse or shame
4. Inadequately motivated antisocial behavior
5. Poor judgment and failure to learn by experience
6. Pathologic egocentricity and incapacity for love
7. General poverty in major affective reactions
8. Specific loss of insight
9. Unresponsiveness in general interpersonal relations
10. Fantastic and uninviting behavior with drink and sometimes without
11. Suicide rarely carried out
12. Sex life impersonal, trivial, and poorly integrated
13. Failure to follow any life plan

These explicit features stand as criteria against which to compare other psychopathic-like syndromes.

Neurotic Psychopathy

Neurotic problems characterized by psychopathic-like acting out are relatively common (cf. Karpman, 1948; McCord & McCord, 1964). Rather than utilizing the defense of repression seen in other neurotic patterns, or perhaps settling on a symbolic ritual, the inner conflict is expressed in the familiar psychopathic behavior pattern. Such persons often show hysterical personality organization, although not especially prone to conversion symptoms. There is likely to be great instability accompanied by self-dramatizing and furious attention seeking. Seductiveness, seemingly unconscious, is likewise characteristic. The childish vanity and egocentrism that is common is accompanied by a blasé disregard of the rights and dignity of others: People are used as objects for extending the ego.

Such a list of symptoms and motives parallels closely those found in our target psychopath. He or she too is egocentric, unconcerned for the rights of others, unstable, and sexually cavalier. Perhaps the single distinguishing mark is that fundamentally neurotic cases do suffer, do experience misery themselves, unlike the psychopath, while, like him, they also create misery for those coming in contact with them. The intrapsychic conflict that exists here, difficult as this may be to confirm, gives another meaning to the neurotic-based psychopathic behaviors than that found in true psychopathy. Karpman has stated this absence of significant psychodynamics in true psychopathy especially starkly: "The psychopath has no conflict [1948, p. 525]."[3] I am indeed not sure a differential diagnosis can be made between the neurotic and the true psychopath short of a longer range look at the person than is common in the clinic, but perhaps I only betray my own diagnostic limitations.[4] For clarity, I have selected for brief discussion several cases that I have known in this longitudinal way in order to give more substance through personal experience to the behavioral nuances displayed. These cases have impressed me as being basically neurotic in nature in spite of noteworthy psychopathic overtones.

THE CASE OF NORA

Nora was an American college student of 21 or 22 years who had both personal and academic difficulties at the time I met her, during a second or third matriculation. In the small-town setting, far from her well-to-do family, she tore a considerable swath via provocative sexual acting out, drug involvement, and exaggerated attention-seeking behaviors. There was a fierce sense of animal energy about her—and at the same time a "street wiseness" about the ways of man. I think I first saw her walking a dog on a cold winter day while conspicuously barefoot, stomping in and out of business places with single-minded aggressiveness and aplomb. Her depredations were considerably enhanced by a pretty face and figure and intelligence which was, I should estimate, at minimum high average. Nora disappeared from town one day, subsequently relating that she had hitch-hiked out west, where she casually took up residence with a married workingman whom she met on the journey. Eventually his wife returned home, which resulted in a raucous parting for Nora, which she related with relish and casual good humor. Returning to the aforementioned campus with a flashy borrowed car she simply "hung around" rather than re-enrolling as a student, continuing

[3] Karpman would remove this group entirely from the designation psychopath, coining for them the term "anethopathy," which he has viewed as a distinct disease. This term and idea have never gained currency.

[4] I find independent confirmation from Jaspers, however. He included the criterion of "an extensive analysis of the case in its phenomenological, meaningful and causal aspects [quoted in Zubin, 1967, p. 380]" in his discussion of diagnosis of the personality disorders.

what seemed a desperate effort to establish some sort of meaningful relationship, while continuing to behave with social abandon. She flitted precariously from one friendship to another, but always in the spotlight of local bars and hangouts, conspicuous in a campus setting where conspicuous behavior was more or less the norm. I recall once seeing her pick up a beer bottle from the bar with her teeth, hold it aloft, and drink from it. Such skills created no small sensation among the all-male crowd in attendance. At such times she displayed notable verbal aggressiveness toward anyone who came in range. This often took the form of provocative flirting responses. On last report Nora had returned to the family home with no clear intentions, except seemingly bent on marriage and family, as she had previously intimated to me.

Discussion with Nora suggested a very ordinary—but not less intense for its ordinariness—desire to love, marry, and fulfill a wifely role. While on the face of it this could be judged a typical search for a magic cure common to nearly all psychological problems, still Nora aimed her efforts at targets worthy of her own potential, rather than the shotgun searching so common in the psychopath. And while artless and contradictory in her style, she seemed able to realistically appraise a potential mate and situation and to give up pursuing him when the likelihood of success was vanishingly small. Her behavior to this extent was calculated. There was not the quixotic, ill-considered, even perverse coupling seen by many professionals as common to the psychopath. I do not mean to say that her sexual behavior itself was rationally contrived, only that it was not perversely random. Also she seemed to suffer in the throes of her chaotic periods, and there was little of the gay, perpetually rebounding psychopath evident. Her most conspicuously outrageous acts had a sense of deadliness about them. She gave a decided feeling of desperate searching for meaning and substance rather than just "passing through life" frivolously. One had the distinct impression that she was salvageable, treatable, although I have no later follow-up information to validate this impression.

THE CASE OF JOHN

A second example was a man with whom I became acquainted when he was in his late twenties. The son of a successful father and attractive, youngish mother, John has managed to earn his baccalaureate degree and for the most part remain actively employed. The writer knew him fairly intimately during a 4-year period when John held a relatively minor administrative post while solidifying a reputation as a playboy bachelor. A classic example of Freud's "phallic man," he was physically attractive and athletic, probably of superior intelligence, and seemed incapable of more than a short, intense "affair" with others. With women the affairs were traditionally sexual and John became easily bored with a succession of women casually met. The male friendships seemed also tinged with sexuality, not only because of their intensity and closeness, but also because of John's tendency to project superhuman qualities on new friends. This might take the form of extolling the friend's unlimited power to attract females, or stories of unmatched sexual prowess—none of which seemed confirmable by others, but told with great gusto.

Affable and modish, John was likeable and popular, with interests best described as current, but seriously lacking in depth. Always expecting the big business break and planning helter-skelter for a future as a rich man, he was quick to tick off a list of important friendships with prominent people for whom he would soon be performing important services. He would evince passion for quick-wealth schemes, from chain letters to fast-food franchises, but a few days after the height of the passion would seem to have trouble remembering the project. His recent work history has been largely confined to bit parts in television advertisements, miscellaneous selling, and serving as man Friday to various film people.

One of John's more fascinating qualities was a seeming inability to communicate a message matter-of-factly. In presenting a topic or idea to another, he would invariably give it an element of allure, an extra polish, as if no bit of information by itself were of sufficient interest; therefore the listener must be lured to it. Perhaps John distrusted his own Being as an "interest getter," and felt that only through dramatizing every communication could he win and hold his audience. One can conjecture that this was a pattern developed from childhood as a competitive device against an equally attractive younger sibling in gaining mother's approval; it is a quality that gave the appearance of an automatic dynamism, turned on without forethought or even specific purpose—seduction for seduction's sake.

What, if anything, separates this charming gay caballero from the true psychopath? The distinction I would argue rests with: (a) the capacity to suffer what seems genuine depression; (b) honesty with others; (c) basically generous impulses.

While not precisely the man to rely on for your own future, e.g., in joint planning to get rich quickly, John at the same time did not seem disposed to sabotage others for the sheer hell of it. Nor to sabotage himself either, for that matter, as we so often see with the psychopath, although poor planning, as mentioned, frequently left him at loose ends. He was also generally frank in pointing out to new girl-friends his disinterest in an exclusive or permanent liaison. Nor did he appear to expect more from another than he gave, little though that might be. Such failures of opportunism would seem to rule him out of the psychopathy diagnosis, in spite of the similarities at various points. The behaviors added up more to a tragic "marketing personality" in Fromm's (1955) sense—in a frantic search for the highest bidder for his charms—and withall lacking the unconscious viciousness that typically flows from the psychopath.

The Delinquent

A dangerous diagnostic tendency has been the cavalier practice of lumping delinquent youth together, labeling them psychopaths or sociopaths, and drawing conclusions about personality variables from data derived from such a mix. Numerous theorists have protested this practice. Hare, for example, has written

> Many individuals exhibit aggressive, antisocial behavior, not because they are psychopathic or emotionally disturbed, but because they have grown up in a delinquent subculture or in an environment that fosters and rewards such behavior [1970, p. 8].

Wiggins (1968) has noted that Peterson, Quay, and their associates have determined the multidimensional nature of delinquency through factor analytic research. In addition to the "psychopathic factor" of impulsivity, rebelliousness, and lack of emotional involvement, another of their delinquent factors was associated with neuroticism and involved personality inventory items reflecting tension, guilt, and discouragement. A third factor suggested failure and incompetence and was labeled "inadequacy" by the investigators. Clausen (1957) argued that many traits ascribed to the psychopath were common among American adolescents reared in slum areas—"inability to form deep and lasting attachments, overvaluation of immediate goals, lack of concern with the rights of others and emotional poverty [p. 267]." Such people are typically not free of anxiety and self-doubt as is the psychopath (Taylor, 1975). Jenkins (1966), in reviewing 500 child guidance clinic cases, found nonpsychopathic delinquents to be socialized to a narrow peer group, rather than being "undomesticated," as were those children whose extreme case was the psychopath.

It is not my intent to put together a comprehensive picture of the delinquent or even various subtypes of delinquency. The point is that delinquent behavior is a manifestation that could flow from as wide a variety of causes or personality types as there are in the broad human spectrum itself. The McCords (1964) say that Sheldon Glueck, after extensive research with United States prison populations, estimated the psychopaths among them at only 20%. Criminal behavior is multi-determined, multifaceted, as these researches underscore.

The Pseudopsychopathic Schizophrenic

That schizophrenia, particularly of Arieti's "stormy" variety (1955), sometimes shows the acting out pattern typical of the psychopath is no news to experienced clinicians, although such a diagnostic label is only "unofficially" used. Hoch (1972) has reminded us to look carefully for a psychotic process in stormy, destructive cases, thereby reinforcing again the concern against diagnosing strictly at the behavioral level. While the subtle clinical symptoms of schizophrenia are frequently overlooked, Hoch states

> Intellectual impairments are always present and should be recognized. In addition to the so-called "semantic dementia" characteristic of the sociopathic individual, typically schizophrenic, concretization, paralogical thinking and circumstantiality are present. In those cases of pseudosociopathic schizophrenia which did not have a psychotic break sufficiently apparent to require the attention of a psychiatrist, the underlying schizophrenic disorder is nonetheless evidenced in the basically autistic and dereistic life approach, the varying degrees of disturbances of affect and interpersonal relationships, and usually in the profusion of pseudoneurotic and antisocial symptomatology present [1972, p. 772].

It is also his opinion that the pseudopsychopathic schizophrenic is more bizarre in his antisocial behavior than is the true psychopath. I interpret him to mean that the acting out of the former is *dominated* by its bizarre quality and reflects more desperation in its expression—the whimsical quality conspicuously missing.

Bender (1959) traced the history of 10 cases judged by her to be pseudopsychopathic schizophrenia. In late childhood these cases already showed various portents of schizophrenia: auditory hallucinations, panic states, body preoccupation, motility disturbances, and paranoid ideation. Behaviorally they also showed delinquency, homosexuality, pyromania, and impulsive, violent reactions. Coming on these cases first in the adult years, one would be easily inclined to reach for a diagnosis of psychopathy. However cases with this kind of early history frequently "mature" to the typical schizoid states of disorganized withdrawal and autism or catatonic responses, according to Bender.

Serious attempts at suicide would be anticipated with the psychotic pseudopsychopath in contrast to the psychopath. Cleckley has observed that it was only after many years of experience with true psychopaths that he encountered an authentic suicide. He considers these cases vitually immune from suicide, in spite of cleverly staged bogus attempts (Cleckley, 1976).

One could include also a discussion of the chronic brain syndromes who act out psychopathically (also sometimes seen in the aftermath of lobotomy), but here the diagnosis is made on a neurological, not psychological, level. Suffice it to say that such cases are readily known in the clinic and may overlap with the acting-out psychotic in the usual ways that chronic brain syndromes and schizophrenia overlap. The usual neurological test battery would be the preferred decision maker in questionable cases. Again, the relationship of such cases to psychopathy is more apparent than real—an epiphenomenon.

That there may be physiological factors predisposing to psychopathic acting out is a hypothesis that has gained renewed vigor over the last decade, on the basis of a growing, if controversial, experimental literature. Such cases would have little in common with the pseudopsychopath who is more likely to have a predominantly schizoid personality organization.

3

The Search for a
Constitutional Explanation

The effort to find something "given" or fixed in the individual as a basis for explaining abnormal behavior has a long and fascinating history. From the very beginning there was an attempt to relate temperament or character to individual constitution. With respect to psychopathic-like behaviors, the history is shorter, but still manages to span several centuries (cf. Sheldon, 1940). The currently disavowed diagnosis "constitutional psychopathic inferiority" was one outgrowth of this effort. The search for this given as an explanatory device continues unabated and carries across what might for classificatory purposes be called genetic, body type, and reaction tendency theories. These approaches are not necessarily independent, although sometimes discussed in the research literature as if they were. Most theorists who have sought for personality in body shape have also discussed reaction potential, as seen in endocrine or cortical functioning, as an important influence on personality development. Reaction potential is a more subtle, less dramatic aspect of the person than his body outline, and does not lend itself to judgments by everyman as does shape. Let us for the moment follow everyman and look briefly at the history of interest in body configuration and personality.

PHYSIQUE AND PSYCHOPATHY

According to Sheldon (1949), Hippocrates designated the two fundamental physical types *phthisic habitus* (long, thin, vertical) and *apoplectic habitus* (short, thick, horizontal), which are paralleled by the more recent designations *asthenic* and *pyknic*. The nineteenth century added a third dimension, *type musculaire* (today's athletic mesomorph), to complete the three basic body types common to modern theory.

This typing attempt carried over into the continental phrenology of Gall and Spurzheim (Davies, 1955). The phrenologists attempted to relate physique dimensions, chiefly involving the shape and size of the cranium, to types of temperament. A temperament or character trait was thought to manifest itself on the basis of the hereditary development of the corresponding brain region. A cranial "bump," e.g., in the "destructiveness region," indicated increased tendencies toward that behavior. Thirty-seven characteristics, give or take a few, could be objectively scaled using, in America, the "Phrenological Self-Instructor" (Bakan, 1966).

With Darwin, Galton, and other scientists of the late nineteenth century, exact anthropometric measurement was born, and when coupled with correlational statistics invented at the same time, permitted more quantitative relating of physique and temperament. What in general filtered out of this early work has been the pairing of the long–thin physique with an intellectual (cerebral) orientation, and short–thick with visceral–gut dominance, and the muscular–square type with activity as primary orientation.

A twentieth-century attempt to relate body type (somatotype) to character predisposition is the work of Ernst Kretschmer (1940), who sought specific morphological characteristics among those who behave abnormally—a relation between body and mental pathology. One of his early observations was that the "circular insanity" of manic depression seemed more characteristic of the pyknic body, while the introverted schizophrenic commonly showed asthenic (leptosome) qualities. Kretschmer also included a dysplastic type, which represented an unsymmetrical mix of the three primary components. He discussed such relevant formulations as the schizoid psychopath and the "sensitive character" (Haefner, 1961).

William Sheldon's (1940) typology relates to that of Kretschmer,[1] but

---

[1] But Sheldon was at pains to point out differences in their systems of classification, noting that while Kretschmer was skillful and consistent in his typing, their three fundamental types were only superficially related. I do not know that Sheldon has clearly documented systematic differences between himself and Kretschmer.

he has been even more quantitative and systematic in his body typing. Working carefully from detailed measurement of cases, he has utilized seventeen body diameters, e.g., of the neck, for determining a somatotype. While he also located three fundamental somatotypes— endomorphy, mesomorphy, echomorphy—he has viewed these as gradable dimensions, not discrete categories. He has used a measurement scale ranging from 1 to 7 to express amount of the three components. Thus a "strong endomorph" might be 6–1–1 or 7–2–2, a strong ectomorph 1–1–7. Sheldon has related these three somatotypes to three basic temperament types—viscerotonia, somatotonia, and cerebrotonia—and found impressive correlations. Mesomorphy, for example, correlated highly with somatotonia ($r = .82$ in an early study), which is characterized temperamentally as assertive, love of adventure, lust for power and domination, love of risk, competitive, callous, ruthless, relatively indifferent to pain, and oriented toward youthful goals and activities. Considering these descriptive adjectives, it would seem likely that we would find diagnosed psychopaths clustering here, and that is what several investigations have indicated. Sheldon found that delinquent youth (400 U.S. males) were elevated on mesomorphy and low on ectomorphy.[2] The Gluecks (1950) used the same basic somatotypes as Sheldon to study 500 delinquents matched against 500 nondelinquent controls matched for age, IQ, residence, and ethnic background. They found a significant preponderance (2:1) of mesomorphs among masculine delinquents, with ectomorphy favoring the nondelinquent controls nearly 3 to 1. Lindzey (1965) reports on a doctoral study by Cortes matching 100 adolescent criminal law violators with an age-matched group having no record of delinquent behavior. Fifty-seven percent of the delinquents compared with 19% of the controls were mesomorphic. Thirty-three percent of the controls against 16% of the delinquents were ectomorphic.

In spite of such support, body type/character type theories from the first half of the twentieth century have found little resonance among recent researchers into psychopathy—or any other diagnosis, for that matter. Prominent reasons range from the stolid commitment to environmentalism that dominates Western theory and research to the frequent slipperiness of body types that have been offered by different

[2] In turning his attention to psychopathic-like delinquency, Sheldon not only shows that a biological commitment such as his is not inherently inflexible, but has come close to the writer's own thesis: "It may be that students of delinquency, failing to take into account the inherent delinquency of institutions, have never got to the heart of delinquency at all [1949, p. 826]." He went on, in discussing this study, to side with the delinquent against his society!

researchers. There is also the perennial problem of the diagnostic categories themselves, and contemporary disaffection with official classification systems. Rosenthal (1970) adds the psychological ground that most of the early work was done by German scientists, and there has been a loathing on the part of non-German researchers to associate with racist material, potentially distillable from this approach if types should match at all to some measure of race. Somatotypes are judged to be inherited, and if temperament correlates regularly occur, then heredity would contribute strongly, for example, to delinquency.

REACTION TENDENCY AND PSYCHOPATHY

Hippocrates, in addition to designating fundamental body types, proposed a theory wherein four body fluids, black and yellow bile, blood, and phlegm, were related to mental disorders such as mania, melancholia, phrenitis, and hysteria. Thus the person predisposed to mania was thought to suffer an excess of black bile in his system. The Roman physician Galen (AD 130–200) proposed a four-way system of temperament: melancholic, phlegmatic, choleric, and sanguine (see Figure 3.1). These traits of temperament were based on Hippocrates' idea of animal spirits flowing through the body, which in their varying amounts and combinations, accounted for varying temperament types. This humoral theory of temperament went on to dominate Western medicine into the Middle Ages. While medical science no longer attributes all physical sickness to "bile imbalance," there are closely related if rather more sophisticated contemporary theories of the effect of, e.g., endocrines on behavioral displays.

Kurt Schneider (1940, 1950) is a biologically oriented theorist whose cataloguing of psychopathic types is prominently discussed in Europe (cf. Haefner, 1961; Kallwas, 1969). His definition of the psychopathic character is based on inborn, constitutional components. Under constitution Schneider has included genetic factors, morphology, and reactive functions. The psychopath is viewed as an *abnormal personality* distinguishable from a psychotic process or transcient personality state. Schneider (1950) takes a dim view of illness defined socially or even psychologically. In anticipation of Szasz's (1960) criticisms, he has noted the hidden value judgments common to these ways of defining normality. Unlike Szasz, however, he has rejected social definitions of illness as being metaphorical and has insisted on a somatic orientation as ultimately the only defensible one. Schneider does not view psychopathy as an organic process, but one with morphologic and

FIGURE 3.1. Diagram showing medieval typology (inner circle) and modern personality description in terms of correlational analysis of trait measurements (outer circle). [Reprinted by permission of John Wiley & Sons, Inc. from Biological basis of personality by H. J. Eysenck in *Theories of Personality: Primary Sources and Research,* edited by G. Lindzey & C. S. Hall. Copyright © 1965 by John Wiley & Sons, Inc.]

functional components within the structure of an abnormal personality, i.e., illustrated through abnormal reactions, which may relate to specific body types. For example, the basic reaction tendencies of Kretschmerian theory—primitive, expansive, sensitive—are recognized as ways of distinguishing subcategories of psychopathy on the basis of given "experience types." Thus the expansive reaction is judged characteristic of the *sthenisch* type. In the extreme case of the "expansive psychopath," there is an *"asthenische Stachel"* or opposite, leptosomic incentive, intrapsychically, resulting in *ueberempfindlichkeit* (oversensitivity). In this type of individual, the outcome is said to be inevitable conflict with society, neurotically or paranoically expressed—the powerless individual against the all-powerful social order. American diagnosticians of today would probably judge some of Schneider's 10 psychopathic subtypes as either fundamentally neurotic, e.g., the "insecure" (*selbstunsichere*) psychopath, or psychotic, e.g., the "fanatic psychopath." While Schneider held to the need to diagnose on a constitutional basis, he was aware that pure types—even as he endeavored to set them out—were rare to find.

In contemporary English language research and theory, there has been an increasing interest in physiological theories of abnormality, in spite of the dominating environmentalist epistemology. Radical empiricism as epistemology tends to couple with the belief that there are no significant differences in individuals that do not come in from the outside environment, hence there are no "real" differences. This assumption is so general that it is typically never called into question by the committed. Nonetheless even empirically oriented researchers have taken to examining differences between individuals in reaction potential as possibly given. Whether inherited or a function of the in utero environment, Sontag (1966) at the Fels Research Institute found individual differences in heart rate and movement already discernible in the fetus. Bell, in an article concerning the socialization process among animal and human young, argued

> Children low in person orientation induce less nurturance from parents, and their behavior is controlled less by variations in social response of parents. They are interested in physical activity and inanimate objects. Their stimulus characteristics primarily mobilize those elements in the parent nurturance repertoires pertaining to providing and withholding physical objects and activities. Since love-oriented control techniques are less useful with these children and material reinforcers cannot always be flexibly applied, their parents more frequently show further recourse to physical punishment [1968, p. 85].

This is an important departure from the faith that the infant is putty to be shaped helter-skelter by forces in his environment and becomes a reckless acter-outer purely on the basis of what has been done to him. To some extent at least, the infant commands and directs parental responses, as cartoonists have pictured the rat as doing in his famous struggle with the experimenter. A child such as Bell projects forces different parental behavior than would a child "moving toward" others.

Hans Eysenck is a methodological behaviorist, but, judging from his interest in the autonomic nervous system (ANS), he is not epistemologically committed to behaviorism. He has been active in searching out physiological roots of psychopathy. His two fundamental dimensions of personality based on ANS reactivity are neuroticism (stability-instability) and introversion–extraversion. (He later added a third dimension—psychoticism.) These were derived from factor analysis of self ratings and various psychological tests (most notably Eysenck's own Maudsley Personality Inventory and later Eysenck Personality Inventory), and permit ordering any individual along the respective primary continua. The psychopath should answer to the adjectives contained in the northeast quadrant of Figure 3.1. He or she is high on extraversion (E), high on neuroticism (N), and low in anxiety.[3]

Eysenck views differences in potential reactivity of the ANS as underlying differences in potential for classical conditioning. The psychopath conditions poorly. He is emotionally labile, low in anxiety, and behaviorally uninhibited, all attributes assumed to make him a poor candidate for the learning of society's permissible behaviors. Eysenck has carried his analysis through to the cortical level, where he initially speculated that the uninhibited behavior of the psychopath and extraverts in general was a function of a rapid rise in cortical inhibition (or neural impulse blocking) with slow dissipation—and maintenance of a relatively high level. He has developed a "tapping test" presumed to measure this cortical inhibition. It consists of having the subject tap a metal plate with a metal stylus as fast as possible. According to the hypothesis an extravert should experience greater performance decrement, the dissipation of which would show in greater reminiscence than for introverted subjects. He found that introverted subjects averaged only one involuntary rest pause during a 1 minute performance, with extraverts averaging 18 (1964)! After a programmed rest pause of 10 minutes following 5 minutes of continuous tapping, psychopathic children showed a much greater improvement than did normal children. Eysenck initially attributed this greater reminiscence effect among the psychopathic children to the dissipation of cortical inhibition. Later (1965b) it was found that introverts and extraverts did not differ significantly in pre-rest performance on simple conditioning tasks where the cortical inhibition hypothesis would have predicted poorer performance for extraverts. Eysenck has abandoned the explanation of reminiscence in terms of dissipation of inhibition in favor of a "theory of consolidation." With this theory a neural fixation process is presumed to continue after the organism is no longer confronted with the learning

[3]Some of the terms casually interchanged and therefore to be aware of in this and subsequent research are "delinquent," "extravert," and "psychopath."

task stimuli. The theory predicts that after rest from a learning task introverts would show greater work decrement than extraverts because of greater conditioned inhibition among this strong and quickly conditioned group.

> As it turned out, the new theory made the same prediction as the old regarding the correlation between extraversion and reminiscence for *short* rests; however, it made quite contrary predictions for *long* rest pauses (Eysenck, 1974), confirming the consolidation theory and in part contradicting the inhibition theory [1974a, p. 308].

Eysenck addresses the psychopath as the proto-typical unstable extravert of Figure 3.1, although he has expanded his discussion of this northeast quadrant to include criminals in general. He has noted that his high extraversion quadrant includes both sociability and impulsiveness components. It is the latter component which he feels bears the major burden of distinguishing control subjects from criminal.

Lykken (1957) set out to test the relationship of anxiety to psychopathic personality. He started from the assumption, not unlike Eysenck's, that psychopaths are defective in their ability to develop conditioned anxiety in the sense of an anticipatory emotional response to appropriate warning signals: They should be poor at learning to avoid an unpleasant stimulus. He used Cleckley's list of criteria to define the primary psychopath and had clinical judges rate prison inmate case histories to determine group placement. Those whose reaffirmed diagnosis remained psychopath, but who still did not match Cleckley's criteria in important respects, he placed in the neurotic psychopath subgroup. He then matched prisoner groups of primary and neurotic psychopaths with a normal (student) group on age and IQ. Lykken found, as predicted, that while normal subjects decreased their shock-rewarded error score over 20 trials to a "mental maze,"[4] the psychopaths showed only slight avoidance conditioning. This was especially true for the primary group, who showed significantly least avoidance of the shock stimulus, with the neurotic group also avoiding less than the students. All three groups scored similarly as regards

---

[4]This consisted of a metal cabinet containing a counter, two pilot lights, and four switches. At each of 20 choice points the subject could advance to the next choice point by pressing one of the arbitrarily correct switches. The ostensible purpose of the test for the subject was that it was a learning task requiring intelligence. If one of the three incorrect switches was pressed the machine did not advance and an error was recorded. Regarding avoidance learning, at each choice point one of the three incorrect switches was arbitrarily programmed to deliver a moderate electric shock. By judiciously choosing, the subject could avoid shock, although he was not instructed nor encouraged to do so.

learning the positively reinforced aspects of the task, so that differences found could be attributed to differences in avoidance learning. It is assumed that avoidance learning is mediated by anxiety, and the failure of the psychopaths to avoid shock was interpreted as a function of the abnormally low anxiety in these individuals.

Schachter used much the same design as Lykken, however he employed only prisoners high, low, and "mixed" on measures of psychopathy. These measures were also modeled largely on Cleckley's criteria, and included in addition number of offenses committed and time spent in prison. Of special interest in this study was the attempt to manipulate arousal by administering adrenaline to the experimental group and a placebo to the control subjects. Adrenaline mimics the action of the sympathetic nervous system. As in Lykken's study, all groups showed similar learning curves to the positively reinforced ("manifest" task) mental maze Lykken had employed. However when the high psychopaths were injected with adrenaline they showed significantly fewer errors in the avoidance of shock (the hidden task). Placebo injection made no apparent difference; Schachter's law psychopathy and "normal criminal" groups showed no such response to the drug. The normals in fact were seemingly adversely affected by the adrenaline and "they do not learn at all [Schachter, 1971, p. 166]." Schachter attributed this discrepancy to the ANS arousal properties of adrenaline and the differential sensitivity of the psychopath to adrenaline.

Quay (1965) is generally credited with formulating the stimulus-seeking or arousal hypothesis. Psychopaths are assumed to have a higher threshold for stimulation (lesser basal reactivity) and to satiate more rapidly to a given stimulus. The psychopath, so goes the theory, is chronically threatened with a boredom to which normally reacting persons are less susceptible. He or she has a problem maintaining an optimal arousal level. Easy boredom and intolerance of monotony then translates into the restless seeking after action, which, depending on environment, could easily lead to delinquent acts. Punishment may fail to deter because the motive is so basic.

Emmons and Webb (1974) selected psychopaths on the basis of MMPI scores and Lykken's Activity Preference Questionnaire. Supporting Quay, they found the psychopaths to be "pathological stimulation seekers" (p. 620) in comparison with normals and acting-out neurotics on the basis of a "sensation-seeking scale." Psychopaths also experienced, on self report, less overall affect in their lives than the other groups. Borkovec (1970) found that psychopathic delinquents defined on the basis of a factored checklist had lower skin conductance measures than did neurotic or normal delinquents. His subjects were positioned on their backs in a dark room, and after an accommodation period of 5 minutes were presented a 1000 Hz tone stimulus 21 times for 1 second duration at 30 second intervals. Borkovec argued, also in consonance with Quay, that the underreactivity of the psychopathic group may come from their "stimulation-less" environment, and that their lowered reactivity is the underlying basis of their poor conditionability. Interestingly, with nude female figures as the stimulus, the responses of the psychopathic delinquents in this all-male study came "up to normal" (1970, p. 222). Scura and Eisenman (1971) classified 60 prisoners on the basis of high and low Psychopathic Deviate (pd) scale scores to the MMPI. High scorers showed less conditioning of a verbal response to negative reinforcement than did low scorers. Sarbin, Allen, and Rutherford (1965) found that persons (delinquents among them) selected on the basis of low scores on Gough's socialization scale were significantly less conditionable than more socialized subjects, even when the latter also included delinquents. Subjects were 16–19 years, white, and male, and reinforcement was verbal approval for a story constructed from small cardboard figures.

Hare has discussed a "cortical immaturity" hypothesis regarding psychopathy and noted that studies, using the electroencephalogram (EEG) as a measure, "have produced rather consistent results [1970, p. 35]." The hypothesis involves EEG patterns as a measure of cortical arousal and is based on the supposition that theta wave activity is normal in young children but relatively infrequent in adults (Gale, 1975). In studying the "positive spike phenomenon" (an EEG tracing of 14 and 6 wave peaks) alleged to be characteristic of psychopathic criminal offenders, Hughes, Means, and Stell (1971) did find significantly more aggressive and impulsive acts among 50 juvenile court cases with the positive spikes than among both 50 normal cases and 35 cases with other EEG abnormalities. They suggest that organic factors may be involved in such behaviors.

EVALUATING THE EVIDENCE FOR CONSTITUTIONAL CORRELATES OF PSYCHOPATHY

A point which has impressed me, since first looking at research tasks designed to show that the psychopath is less "socially appropriate" regarding stimuli to which he is experimentally introduced, is how irrelevant, silly, and boring many such stimuli are. An uncommitted outsider might judge that it would be to the psychopath's credit if he indeed gave such stimuli, e.g., a standard EEG exam, a 1000 Hz tone, short shrift. Both conditioning theory and arousal theory hold that there is reduced responsiveness—either to a stimulus signaling a mildly aversive event (conditioning theory), or underarousal (or rapid habituation and consequent underarousal) to repeated laboratory stimulation. Eysenck's tapping test, for example, could hardly be called everyman's excitement. In commenting on EEG findings in a recent review Gale echoed this judgment:

> Now in such circumstances, if the psychopath is indeed already low aroused, and if indeed he also couldn't care a damn about what the experimenter wants, he could easily drift off into light sleep, whereas psychotic and anxiety state patients may be so distressed by the testing environment and so confused by the need to obey an impossible instruction, that they find it impossible to relax at all. For this latter group, anxiety induced by the experimental laboratory could *diminish* the incidence of naturally occurring slow wave activity. Thus, in psychopaths studied, incidence of theta could be artificially elevated, while theta in other, more anxiety prone groups could be artificially diminished [1975, p. 10].

Recall also that Borkovec is the study previously cited (1970) found that his psychopathic male delinquents responded normally on skin conductance measures when the stimuli were nude female figures and not a 1000 Hz tone. Schmauk (1970) found that psychopaths can learn to avoid punishment as well as a normal control group does when the punishment is appropriate to their value system. In his study it is not surprising that money was a more effective reinforcer than was aversive stimulation with the psychopaths.

The importance of comparable controls in EEG studies is emphasized in Gale's (1975) observation that long-term confinement, with its wrenching boredom, could also significantly alter brain wave activity. In a recent study of electrocortical responses where 27 male sociopaths were matched for age and sex with noninstitutionalized controls, Syndulko, Parker, Jens, Maltzman, and Ziskind (1975) found, among other negative results, no significant differences between groups on EEG "power spatial density" or in overall contingent negative variation (CNV) amplitude or topography. The experimental cases here were selected on the basis of both objective tests and psychiatric interview. In his review Gale found the bulk of over 100 studies exploring EEG correlates of psychopathy grossly inadequate:

> The problem with the studies of psychopathy and the EEG reviewed by Ellingson, and which characterizes most if not all subsequent studies is that the investigators assume (i) that psychopaths are a *type*, (ii) that they constitute a *homogeneous* group,

(iii) that this group is characterized by *brain pathology,* (iv) that the "abnormal" EEG has functional significance, and (v) that the EEG reflects *biological* predisposition to certain behaviors [1975, p. 6].

One significant problem pointed out by Gale is that "atypical" EEGs are common among an unselected youthful population, registering perhaps as high as 25%. Then too, normal controls on occasion show more symptoms, e.g., more positive spike, than do patient groups. "Atypical" patterns are also frequent among other traditional categories of abnormality, so that one must wonder what a typical pattern is. There is low agreement as to what constitutes an abnormal EEG pattern.

With respect to the "cortical immaturity" or "maturational lag" hypothesis, as he has called it, Gale has pointed out the tenuous nature on which it rests, even if and when present:

> The maturational lag hypothesis in its crudest form merely calls upon the observa-
> tions that (i) slow activity appears naturally in children but not in adults, (ii) exces-
> sive slow activity appears in young psychopaths but diminishes with age, (iii)
> psychopathic episodes diminish with age. This is essentially an imputation of cause
> from correlation and is in no sense an explanation since the functional significance of
> the abnormalities is not understood. . . . What is more, it seems strange to talk of
> "maturational lag" in children who tend, if anything, to be physically advanced on
> other criteria, as shown in the well-known Glueck and Glueck study (1956) [1975, pp.
> 28–29].

In spite of the generally negative tone of his review, Gale does not want to count the EEG out as a research tool into psychopathy. He does hold that psychopaths are abnormally low in arousal, in keeping with Quay, and that they can be expected to be "stimulus seeking" in the environment. Individual EEGs can be synchronized with presentation of stimuli to measure stimulus hunger, he argues. He and various coworkers are extending this sort of research to the interpersonal realm through analysis of eye contact responses, vigilance tasks, and corre-lated EEG patterns. Still, he views predictions of behavior based on EEG records as extremely risky because of the overlapping of distribu-tions of EEG patterns and of diagnoses of abnormality. Furthermore, even should careful research turn up consistent substantial correlations between those earning the label psychopath on behavioral or attitudinal measures and EEG activity, it cannot be assumed that the brain activity is the cause of the behavior or attitudes expressed. Attribution of such one-way effects would far overstep the reality of experimental settings.

Eysenck's prominent theory already discussed has also suffered heavy attack in recent years, following considerable research. As indi-cated, the theory originally held that psychopaths should be high on extraversion because of cortical inhibition, high on neuroticism measures, and low in anxiety. In a recent exchange over the Eysenckian theory of delinquency in the *Bulletin of the British Psychological Society,* Cochrane concluded

> The results of 9 separate studies lead Hoghughi and Forrest to the following conclusions. First, that the weight of the evidence shows that young offenders tend to be more *introverted* than normative samples or control groups. Second, delinquents are shown to be more neurotic than comparison groups, but, it is suggested, some part of this may be due to the increased anxiety of delinquents upon being removed from home and placed in a somewhat threatening new situation [1974, p. 20].

In reply Eysenck (1974b) cited unpublished data collected by both Maclean and S. Eysenck where prisoners and nonprisoner controls were matched for age and social class. The prisoners had significantly higher scores on P (psychoticism), E (extraversion), and N (neuroticism), as had been predicted. Taylor, in the same journal, not only judged the theory wanting in general research support but chastised Eysenck for neglecting evidence from his own institute:

> It should also be said that the theory might not have appeared so attractive had Eysenck referred to Field's research (1960) that was conducted under his own general direction, and was published four years before his own book. From this extensive study of conditionability in several different groups of prisoners and other controls, Field uncovered "no conclusive evidence for constitutional or personality deficiencies which can explain crime" (*ibid.,* p. 16). The theory might also have been less widely accepted had Eysenck paid closer attention to Warburton's data that he reported in support of his case (Eysenck, 1964, pp. 123–4). Warburton said that his group of 38 psychopathic prisoners gave "the overall impression . . . that they are chiefly anxious extraverts", but my later calculation of their second order factors merely confirmed their anxiety but *not* their extraversion (cf. Taylor, 1968). Warburton himself conceded his "impressionistic" error . . . [Taylor, 1975, p. 286].

Finally Eysenck may have had, for the time being at least, the last word in replying to Taylor:

> I would not like to give the impression that there have not been advances in the original rather crude theory. The two major components of extraversion—impulsiveness and sociability—appear to bear a differential burden in discriminating criminals from controls, with impulsiveness being much more important; this did not form part of the original theory. It is of particular interest because recent work (Eysenck & Levey, 1972) has shown that the correlation between extraversion and conditioning, too, is mediated almost entirely through impulsiveness rather than through sociability. This would seem to support the original hypothesis that socialized behavior was produced through some form of Pavlovian conditioning. The addition of psychoticism as an important personality factor determining psychopathic and criminal actions is another step in the formulation of a more satisfactory theory (Eysenck, 1970) [Eysenck, 1975, p. 355].

Perhaps the theory is serving to be refined as Eysenck says, but certainly its value for pinpointing psychopathy is attenuated when a hypothesized group is higher on both neuroticism and psychoticism—categories which Eysenck had elsewhere found discrete. While there is research support for the poor conditionability of the psychopath (e.g., Lykken, 1957; Schachter, 1971; Scura & Eisenman, 1971), there is serious doubt about the presence of extraversion, anxiety, and even more unsettling—arousal (Cauthen, 1972; Raskin, 1975; Schachter, 1971). The reason the latter is difficult to delimit is hinted at by Shagass and Overton (1975), who have noted how varying stimulus intensity can alter somatosensory recovery phases following evoked cortical responses. With ulnar nerve stimulation, patients with personality disorder and those functionally psychotic generally showed lower recovery function than nonpatients, but if the stimulus is lessened in intensity with low-recovery subjects, there is typically facilitation of recovery of function. It would seem that one cannot talk about excitability in the abstract. Even such "objective stimuli" as light flashes can be varied to provide varying levels of excitability, and the organism in his natural setting with meaningful stimuli is assuredly more variable, more involved with his stimulus world. This may well account for Borkovec's (1970) skin conductance change when nude figures replaced a 1000 Hz tone. Steinberg and Schwartz (1976) found that while young psychopaths showed no reliable alteration of skin resistance responses following a simple instruction to use affective imagery to elevate this response, they were able to match a control group on heart rate increase. The researchers point out the danger of viewing physiological arousal in the abstract and as a physiological deficit in psychopaths. The psychopath is a selective responder (cf. Schmauk, 1970) and not the humble, invariably "good" subject: The laboratory world is not exactly his oyster.

To me, it seems that the distinction between primary and neurotic psychopathy discussed in the last chapter must be fully considered when obtaining dependent variable measures. The best research designs make some effort to incorporate this distinction (cf. Lykken, 1957; Schachter, 1971). Thus the neurotic or pseudopsychopathic schizophrenic, when casually lumped with the "true variety" on the basis of such gross measuring devices as the Pd Scale of the MMPI (Scura & Eisenman, 1971; Cauthen, 1972), would, not surprisingly, reflect higher anxiety and lesser extraversion than the latter, as Cochrane and Hare suggested might have occurred with Eysenck's delinquents. Hare, indeed, sees the true psychopath as a "stable extravert" (1970, p. 63), and has suggested that Eysenck has perhaps caught largely the neurotic subgroup because of the high ANS lability projected. We have seen, however, that this reactivity issue is a disputed one at present.

It is perhaps appropriate also to mention the chromosomal abnormality designated "the 47, XYY male" and its potential effect on aggressive and antisocial behavior. These men have a doubling of the chromosome relevant to masculine behaviors. Much of the stir raised by this syndrome was occasioned in America by the murder of eight student nurses by a man subsequently shown to have this extra male chromosome, as well as other secondary features of what was quickly labeled a "criminal" type. He also had a long history of criminal offenses. Corroboratively it was then popularly alleged that the percentage of these cases found in mental and penal institutions was significantly greater than in the population at large—approximately 2.3% to .4%, respectively.

Optimism that such violent offenders might be pre-identified by karyotyping and physical criteria (e.g., height over 6 feet, tendency to acne) gave way rapidly under sober review to the observation that by far the majority of violent males had no such chromosomal anomaly, and some who have it produce no noteworthy violence. As Owen observed:

> One of the most widely discussed hypotheses about 47, XYY males is that supernumary Y chromosomes predispose the holder to violent acts of masculine aggression. What began as a reasonable hypothesis—but immediately failed to gain statistical support—was accepted uncritically by an apparently alarming number of practitioners [1972, p. 210].

Owen further reported a study by Griffith *et al.* (1970) in which no differences were found between 47, XYY's and control cases on Eysenck's personality Inventory scales of psychoticism or neuroticism. On the contrary, five XYY's scored lower on the Extraversion scale than did their controls. Even the early incidence statistics have been found wanting. For one thing it has not been possible to identify individual chromosomes without subjective error. Also, early (1965) high incidence rates in institutions were not replicated among institutions later (1970) surveyed. Finally, *presumed* rates among the United States population at large have been less than those subsequently found empirically (Owen, 1972). This does not rule out the potential predisposition such cases may have toward violence; those whose environment does not call it forth would escape its consequences and miss a census based on inmate figures. Owen concluded his survey:

> In the case of 47, XYY males, little can be concluded from the data at hand about phenotypic characters more likely to result from XYY than XY sex chromosomes. Nor

are we in a position to assess the 47, XYY constitution's contribution to phenotypic variance for any characteristic [1972, p. 228].

SUMMARY

It cannot be said that there has been a neglect of constitutional or physiological factors in the search for the roots of psychopathy. True, somatotype theories have suffered neglect since roughly 1950, even though the work of Sheldon and associated criminologists has produced evidence relating mesomorphy and delinquency which, if it were based on theory more acceptable to the dominating climate in social science, would be either (a) embraced as a major contribution to understanding crime; or (b) challenged with carefully controlled research efforts. Instead the theory seems to have fallen fallow.

An exception is Lindzey (1965), who has recapitulated a number of earlier positive studies relating somatotype to criminal behavior. Comparing this work to Sheldon's ideas, he noted that whereas no one is likely to argue that mesomorphy causes criminal behavior, the association is both strong and consistent. The research by Lykken and Schachter reviewed here led him to remind us of Sheldon's characterization of the somatotonic temperament as low in anxiety and indifferent to pain.

As late as 1970, Rosenthal, active in biological research in abnormality, raised again the issue of mesomorphy as a potential hereditary factor in psychopathy. Citing the Gluecks' previously mentioned findings of mesomorphy among delinquents, and arguing that somatotypes are inherited, he concluded that one element at least of behavior variance in psychopathy has a hereditary base. However three other factors included in his analysis in support of the inheritance of psychopathy—high EEG abnormalities, low IQ, and higher XYY types among criminals, as seen in our examination here—do not hold much promise after research scrutiny. This is not to imply that somatotype theories are superior. Sheldon has been critized for inadequate research designs which do seem to have contributed to producing inflated relationships (cf. Anastasi, 1958).

Neglect, too, has certainly not been the fate of Eysenck's hypotheses regarding antisocial behavior. As a theory of criminality, it seems to sin by including too much, and thereby obscures important distinctions that many other investigators have found essential, e.g., that between primary and secondary psychopathy. The theory has suffered some heavy criticisms and basic modifications. An example is the rejection of the idea of *improved* performance among extraverts because of reminiscence regarding a laboratory task in favor of an explanation involving *poorer* performance of the introvert group because of conditioned inhibition. Also, confirmatory data enumerated above seem less conspicuous than negative results in associating extraversion and conditionability with variously defined psychopathic offenders. Further, Eysenck speaks largely to the theory of criminality in general, and the impact then to a biological theory of psychopathy is attenuated. Jenkins (1966), for example, not only found the two distinct types "undomesticated children" and "socialized delinquents" when he computer-clustered the symptoms of his 500 child guidance clinic cases, but he was able to find basic family background differences as well. The backgrounds of the undomesticated children featured prominently an unstable mother who failed to socialize the child and in extreme cases produced a psychopathic personality. Prominent with socialized delinquents was parental neglect, notably by the father, leading in the extreme case to a narrowly socialized, peer-group dominated delinquent.

Eysenck's addition of the factor of psychoticism as basic to many criminal acts is a further widening of the basic "givens" of his theory. Such a change contributes only to theoretical imprecision, unless this factor can be clearly related to a specific subtype of criminal. And here is the rub: By broadening to "criminal" from the already imprecise "psychopath," the theory inevitably must include neurotic and psychotic offenders, who even if they display selected characteristics of the broadened theory, at the same time give little help in early warning systems for crime. Hare has pointed out the danger here:

> One of the difficulties with terms such as secondary and neurotic "psychopathy" is that they imply individuals so labelled are basically psychopaths. However, this is likely to be misleading because the motivations behind their behavior, as well as their personality structure, life history, response to treatment, and prognosis, are very different from those of the psychopath [1970, p. 8].[5]

The hypothesis of underarousability or stimulus seeking accepted by Quay, Hare, Eysenck, Petrie (1967), and others has gained uneven research support. It is not difficult to assume, when one reads the often startling case histories of classic psychopaths, that the psychopath may be unusually susceptible to promises of thrills and excitement, and the fact of his or her often leading the way in seeking the novel and even bizarre gives case history credibility to this laboratory analogue. The

[5]This and subsequent quotations cited to Hare, 1970 are reprinted by permission of John Wiley & Sons, Inc. from *Psychopathy: Theory and Research* by R. D. Hare. Copyright © 1970 by John Wiley & Sons, Inc.

difficulty inherent in obtaining agreement regarding the parameters of stimulus variables such as stimulus intensity, and dependent measures such as varying recovery cycles of evoked cortical potentials (cf Vaughan, 1975), serve as a reminder that theory is easier to posit than confirm. What confirmatory studies cry out for, as Gale (1975) has so strongly advocated, are comparisons with control subjects from the population at large, and ideally from other cultures as well. Schachter's (1971) more dramatic conclusions emphasize these weaknesses. He has attempted to account for his reported discrepancy of high heart rate and seemingly insufficient adrenaline among his psychopaths on the basis of inappropriate labeling. That is, he has argued that the psychopath is not indifferent to his environment as commonly assumed, but is actually more "turned on" than are normals. Precisely because of his over-reactivity in general, he is no more alert to times, e.g., of danger, than to tranquil events; thus he gets into social trespass problems. An experimental analogue would be that instead of suffering sensory deprivation because of a dearth of stimulation, the senses are masked by monotonous stimuli, which, like white noise, gives an equally monotonous effect. Unfortunately Schachter's conclusion was based on only eight cases in contradicting findings of underarousal, and this finding has gained later support (Cauthen, 1972; Raskin, 1975), but it is not unequivocal (Waid, Orne, & Wilson, 1976). Schachter defined normals in his study merely as prisoners who were high on either one or none of the measures he used to define psychopathy! While intriguing, the study needs repeating with an appropriate nonconfined control sample.

Hare (1970) following Ax (1962) has hypothesized that if the psychopath is underaroused, his higher ANS centers may be narcissistically preoccupied or even inadequately functioning and

> [he] may be unable to create the "empathic hypotheses" needed to simulate another's feelings. The implication hence is that the psychopath's lack of empathy may be associated with an inability to give the appropriate autonomic responses to the suffering and distress of others and to situations involving the interpersonal exchange of love, affection, cruelty, and so forth [Hare, 1970, p. 49].

On the surface this reasoning makes good sense psychologically; if one lacks feeling for another one could only with some difficulty take the other's perspective. Schachter's thinking is relevant here insofar as he sees the psychopath as being unable to differentiate a properly exciting circumstance from a routine one, thus his general "over-readiness" is "almost the equivalent of no reactivity at all [1971, p. 179]."

Lurking behind such judgments is a materialistic solution to the mind–body problem favoring physiology. Thus reality is embedded in the state of the body, and feeling is defined as autonomic response:

> If almost every event provokes strong autonomic discharge, then, in terms of internal autonomic cues, the subject feels no differently during times of danger than during relatively tranquil times [Schachter, 1971, p. 179].

There is little hint of a possible reality in the psychological side to feeling. The question persists as to the possibility of having a "feeling" at odds with one's ANS state. The frequently found poor correlations between subjective and objective indices of anxiety, for example, suggest that it is indeed possible. The nature of pain is another puzzle as shrouded in mystery as is anxiety. Without pretending to be able to answer the sphinx-like riddle of the mind–body relation, one can at least turn a searchlight on unwritten premises and thereby point in the direction that a given presupposition should take us. Taking up the Ax–Hare hypothesis, one might expect that the treatment of psychopathy could be furthered with "training of the ANS" to respond appropriately to display of emotions in another, or to generally agreed-on emotional stimuli. The use of biofeedback information of ANS function would seem to be a logical step in treating psychopathy from this perspective.

The EEG research has been ambiguous, correlational, and better executed on the negative (findings) side than the positive, according to Gale (1975). While EEG abnormalities may prove a consistent finding for the habitually violent, he notes "it is questionable whether such individuals are 'psychopaths' within the normal definition of the term [1975, p. 37]."

Further: "This review comes to the unusual conclusion that psychopaths are *not* characterized by an abnormal EEG and that the belief that they are so characterized is a psychopathological myth [1975, p. i]."

We could end this general review of the physiological exploration of correlates of psychopathy on a similar negative note. To date, theory, instruments, and research and its interpretation do not allow the emergence of a coherent picture of psychopathy. However blame is not to be laid casually at the feet of physiological researchers. Many workers in this area are not blind to the seeming "scatter effect" of psychological factors on physiological variables. Vaughan has recently emphasized this problem as seen in relating perceptual variables to recovery cycles of visual evoked responses:

> Correlative studies that employ arbitrary physiological measures without suitable psychological validation cannot yield interpretable results. They do not necessarily depict any physiological correspondence [1975, p. 354]."

Unfortunately, too, physiologically committed researchers rarely look out at the society in which they conduct their studies.

If it is found that in the reaction potential of those designated psychopathic there are factors based on cortical or endocrine anomalies that predispose them toward social trespass, what then? Today's social trespass may be tomorrow's acceptable response, and shadings in this very direction in America from midcentury will concern later chapters of this book. Tayler (1975) has pointed out how unfortunate it would have been to have acted precipitously on Eysenck's early theory regarding intervention to counteract delinquency with pharmacological agents. There is no theory of abnormality which is sufficiently predictive to pass so rigorous a test, nor is there likely to be. To think that there will be is to take society as a constant and to commit oneself to the premise that the major ground for behavior variance is within the individual.

Are those who trespass necessarily in error? We might ask how trespassers compare on the various measures of psychopathy with noninstitutionalized groups, e.g., successful entrepreneurs. Are those who might have similar potential reactions, but do not become marked as trespassers, saved by social class or some other protection?[6] In the ensuing pages we will look at social role theory explanations of psychopathy, and at theory and research that pose a challenge to the very idea that psychopathy invariably represents deviance. Such an approach would not begin to anticipate simple one-to-one relations between some physiological state and the label "psychopath."

[6] An indication is given by Zuckerman, Bone, Neary, Mangelsdorff, and Brustman's (1972) sensation-seeking college men and women, who showed impulsive, nonconforming tendencies, and also scored high on the MMPI Pd Scale. The researchers noted: "The true sensation seeker will tire of any fixed mode of sensation and look for something else. His motive is not necessarily a sick one. When he applies himself to work he tends to be creative. His preference for complex designs is one sign of this [p. 320]."

4

Social Role/Learning Theory
Formulations of Psychopathy

In sharp contrast to those who seek the key to abnormality in body states stand those who view the person as an outcome of his specific experiences of life. One variant of the latter view was broached in Chapter 1, where the emphasis of learning theorists on the reinforcement history of the "deviate" as the major determination of his or her deviation was discussed. Persons behave crazily because they have been rewarded and/or punished in a crazy, perhaps inconsistent, fashion for their behaviors. As previously noted, these theorists prefer psychopath designations such as that of sociopath, or the more recently official category "Antisocial Personality," which emphasize social factors as basic to "deviant" behaviors.

What might occur in producing these sociopaths, so goes the theory, is that for them, other persons in their reinforcing community fail to become acquired reinforcers. That is, for incipient sociopaths, other persons have not taken on appropriate reinforcement value from childhood, so that they are not able to be controlled by the relationship between them and those others (Ullmann & Krasner, 1969). Nonsociopaths, conversely, are presumed to be strongly influenced by the behaviors of others who, functioning as dispensers of reward and punishment, have successfully trained them to emit appropriate social responses. Something in the sociopath's social training is missing, so that the basic steps to full socialization have not been traversed.

Mention was made in Chapter 1 of Buss's discussion of various family triangles which are thought capable of producing psychopathic off-spring. That discussion brought Buss's speculations under the Freudian umbrella because of such constructs as "failure to achieve identification" and recognition of "abnormal personality features" (Buss, 1966, p. 431). Ullmann and Krasner (1969) concentrate on the input side of Buss's analysis. In learning terms the cold, distant qualities of the sociopath come from imitation of a parent who is cold and distant to the child. The child models the powerful but uninvolved parent and this translates to his or her learning the formal requirements of social situations, but no actual involvement in those situations. Another aspect or derivation from the theory involves reinforcement inconsistency. These inconsistent behaviors on the part of the parents

> make it difficult for the child to learn a definite role model, with the result that a consistent self-concept does not develop. The parents reward both "superficial conformity" and "underhanded nonconformity." Because the parent behaves arbitrarily and inconsistently, punishment is the result, but it is unpredictable. Therefore, the child learns how to avoid blame and punishment rather than how to differentiate right from wrong. A frequently observed behavior is that of a child either lying to avoid punishment or making superficial responses such as, "I'm sorry and I won't do it again." The child has then been rewarded for escaping punishment without feeling guilt [Ullmann & Krasner, 1969, p. 454].

Maher's (1966) theory of psychopathy takes a similar turn. The potential psychopath may have a parent who forestalls or reduces punishment for an act of petty thievery, for example, when the child promises not to repeat this behavior. The child then learns to vouchsafe repentance in order to avoid punishment, but not to attach the fear of punishment to the forbidden acts themselves. The indulgence of such a child, who is usually "cute," produces an adult who lacks frustration tolerance and ability to wait for long-term goals. This attractive child comes to associate parental love not with himself, but with his looks or appeal. "A child who has been protected from distress will have no basis for interpreting it in others when he sees it [1966, p. 217]." The behavioral emphasis of the analysis stands out: If it is not personally experienced, it cannot be "felt."

Ullmann and Krasner (1969) say the young psychopath frequently finds himself in situations where "his behavior is treated as if it were *inconsequential* [1969, p. 454; italics in original]." Because of this they say the effects of his behavior are unpredictable for him, and so he has difficulty learning about himself, although "'Where such training in eliciting feedback is provided—in making amends, in being charming—the person later to be called psychopathic learns very well indeed [1969, p. 454]." They conclude that his behavior is inconsequential and he can therefore ignore certain social stimuli because they will provide him no "payoff" anyway in attention. In short, lack of consistent reinforcement means lack of corrective feedback, which means an "unsocialized," quixotic character.

Yet another possibility treated by Ullmann and Krasner (1969) is the predelinquent child from an impoverished environment who has been on the receiving end of severe physical punishment from unsympathetic parents. Again it is assumed that such punishment is likely to be on a random schedule as far as the child is concerned (but in keeping with the moods of the reinforcer), and that there is little he can do to control interpersonal situations in general. This may lead to chronic avoidance behavior by the child.

We have looked at the evidence concerning capacity of psychopaths and delinquents to be conditioned in the laboratory (Chapter 3) and found the interpretation of the results equivocal. Behavior theorists too would doubtless recognize the tentative nature of results obtained with finger shocks in learning a maze when extrapolated to red-blooded psychopaths making a shambles of a company or clinic. The inevitable problem involves the difficulty of the laboratory as an analogue to the environment—with the latter the psychopath can at least anticipate exciting payoffs beyond the laboratory doors.

Up to this point in their theorizing, Ullmann and Krasner have provided some intuitively appealing ad hoc explanations of how psychopaths evolve. However they have moved into vastly more opaque waters when tackling the presumed difference between the impact others have on us normally socialized beings and the impact of this same community on the psychopath. The issue is essentially as follows. It is generally accepted that the psychopath grows up deprived of self-correcting input from others, perhaps seeing his own behavior as inconsequential in controlling situations where others are involved, or when the child experiences the arbitrariness of power figures, he perceives others as being irrelevant. How is it that the psychopath is nonetheless so impressively skillful in seeming to know precisely what others want and how to control and manipulate them. The psychopath has the ability to make other people feel they are getting what they want from him even though the converse is true. That is, the psychopath seems to be very "consequential" for others. The hint given above is that the prepsychopath somehow learns to be charming but this does not translate to learning to perform up to social expectations. Many commentators do naively gloss over the paradox of the psychopath's "social stupidity," or failed conditioning, on the one hand, and the outspoken interpersonal cleverness on the other by blithely counting him or her in with those who are inadequate role players per se. Ullmann and Krasner also enter the murky area of role theory in constructing an explanation of the contradictions psychopathy seems to represent. Let us follow them there, but begin by first examining role theory itself as it has been employed to explain psychopathic behavior.

SOCIAL ROLE THEORY AND THE PSYCHOPATH

Gough (1948) has formulated a theory of psychopathy which has found a ready audience among psychologists and is frequently quoted in discussions of the why and wherefore of this syndrome, particularly by behaviorally inclined theorists. Gough has acknowledged his debt to sociologist G. H. Mead[1] in providing the general theory for his model of psychopathy, which runs briefly as follows. The psychopath is viewed as pathologically deficient in role-playing skills. It is exactly this role playing that is deemed essential in making one sensitive in advance to the reaction of others. This is accomplished in the appropriately social being, according to Mead, through the mediation of these very "others":

> The principle which I have suggested as basic to human social organization is that of communication involving participation in the other. This requires the appearance of the other in the self, the identification of the other with the self, the reaching of self-consciousness through the other [1934, p. 253].[2]

It is here that the psychopath bares his inadequacy: He cannot judge his own behavior from another's point of view.

> First of all, the basis for individual sociality is social interaction, and this interaction is effective in so far as the individual can look upon himself as an object or can assume various roles. This role-taking ability provides a technique for self-understanding and self-control. Learned prohibitions (and all social interdictions must be learned) may be observed by "telling one's self not to behave in a certain way" [Gough, 1948, p. 363].

[1] Guterman (1970) says that Gough's Socialization scale is based on Mead and primarily measures social approval.

[2] This and subsequent quotations cited to Mead, 1934 are reprinted with permission of The University of Chicago Press from *Mind, Self, and Society* by G. H. Mead. Copyright 1934 by The University of Chicago Press.

The psychopath cannot grant the justice of punishment, indeed is frequently dismayed by it (cf. Cleckley, 1955, 1964, 1976), since he cannot take the role of that most important other, the generalized other, i.e., society proper. Society has not "entered the self," the self hence has not gained full consciousness. Again Gough:

> In Mead's terminology this role-taking gradually becomes integrated into a number of self-conceptions, each of which is called a "me," each corresponding to the definition of the self by others. During this developmental period the child will often talk to himself as others talk to him. In time a certain communality and consistency in the patterns permit the evolvement of a conception of the "generalized other," which represents social reality as seen by the self [1948, p. 362].

The psychopath, it is finally argued, suffers a failure of empathy; he cannot "fit into the shoes" of another.

This, in basic outline, is Gough's formulation with roots in Mead. It is an intuitively appealing explanation that has the virtue of being not only succinct but also psychologically cogent. That this seemingly strange, quixotic human we label psychopathic may be at base a social cripple, empathically stunted so that he does not really know what his world wants of him, appeals to the clinician in all of us. At the same time, however, the formulation contains some slippery and uneasy constructs, especially for those looking at abnormality from the behavioral standpoint. There are, after all, terms here such as "participation in the other," "self consciousness," and the bugaboo—empathy. Role-taking itself as viewed by Mead seems to have a meaning with considerable surplus value, empirically speaking (McCorquodale & Meehl, 1948), over and above that which we might lightly (and behaviorally) suppose:

> Role-taking in Mead's terms was an internal, imaginative activity not to be confused with role-playing or psychodramatic methods in which roles are enacted on a stage, nor with the enactment of social roles in real life situations. Mead referred to inner processes of imagination and fantasy [p. 80]. . . . It is true that Mead considered role-taking to be more of a cognitive than an emotional phenomenon [Katz, 1963, p. 77].[3]

Critique of Social Role Theory

Some would say that Mead's granting of sovereign importance to the group in the formation of the self concept gives an exaggeratedly one-

---

[3]Reprinted with permission of Macmillan Publishing Co. from *Empathy, Its Nature and Its Uses* by R. L. Katz. © 1963 by The Free Press.

sided picture of the nature of self. In discussing development of the individual he argued

> Thus he becomes not only self-conscious but also self-critical; and thus, through self-criticism, social control over individual behavior or conduct operates by virtue of the social origin and basis of such criticism . . . this sort of censorship or criticism of himself by the individual is reflected also in all other aspects of his social experience, behavior, and relations . . . social control, so far from tending to crush out the human individual or to obliterate his self-conscious individuality, is, on the contrary, actually constitutive of and inextricably associated with that individuality; for the individual is what he is, as a conscious and individual personality, just in so far as he is a member of society, involved in the social process of experience and activity, and thereby socially controlled in his conduct [1934, p. 255].

In the broadest sense it must be true that the individual's relation to his social group defines him as a person, but any sense that there might be an internal, unique source of energy in the form of autonomous ego strength (Hartmann, 1951), for example, seems to be conspicuously missing in Mead. Another aspect of internal energy, that pertaining to libido, is also underplayed in favor of the crucial role of language in forming Mead's concept of self. What notice Mead gives to Freud is primarily for his concept of the psychological censor as a social control mechanism.

This one-sided emphasis on the power and importance of the social group has the unfortunate consequence—a fallout perhaps not at all intended by Mead—of championing conformity at the expense of individuality (cf. Mead, 1934, p. 162). Butler, in discussing the development of consciousness through a comparison of Hegel and Freud, has noted that self-realization on the basis of internalizing one's society may be seen as politically reactionary (1976, p. 516). From such perspectives the psychopath would be guilty of breaching social etiquette, since he is the individualist personified. More generally, many theorists who champion "rugged individualism"—the so-called objective psychology of novelist Ayn Rand comes immediately to mind—would likely take a dim view of this heavy emphasis on the importance of the other in defining the self, and, as in Mead's formulation, as the basis for judging the psychological health of any person.

The Gough–Mead analysis also ignores the mores of the over-arching culture and its molding effect in the direction of a modal cultural personality (Inkeles & Levinson, 1969). While the psychopath may not be socially integrated in the sense of being a submerged group member, it is by no means clear that he or she is less capable of getting on adequately—or even doing very well—in a culture geared to his or her constellation of psychological traits: The opposite is more likely true.

Mead's hypothesis regarding the power of the group to influence the self-concept has been explored by Cavior and Dokecki (1971). Four groups of American school children, two formed of mutual acquaintances and two composed of students unacquainted with the others, independently ranked pictures of the two mutual-acquaintance groups for physical attractiveness from least to most. Each child from the acquainted groups was also asked where he or she thought his or her peers would rank him or her on this attractiveness dimension. Each child of the acquainted groups also ranked his own picture among his group, and the researchers used this rating as the measure of self-concept. They reasoned that if others are so important to how we define ourselves, the children should have ranked themselves much as their peers did and further that the opinions of peers should correlate highly with the judgments each subject expected from his peers. Results indicated that there were high correlations (average $r = .82$) between self-ratings and classmate rankings as predicted, but the ranking expected from others by the subjects was not significantly correlated with how he or she was in fact ranked. The latter correlation was no higher than that between his or her own self-rank and measures of his or her attractiveness by those groups of students who were totally unknown to him or her. Insofar as the self-concept is thought to be a function of how significant others shape us through feedback of their attitudes, Mead's view was not supported; the expected rank was unrelated to the actual rank awarded by known others. On the other hand, it is questionable if the measure of self-concept can be delimited to physical attractiveness—even among fifth graders the "self" assuredly has many other dimensions. Although high, the correlations between self-ratings and classmate ratings are too ambiguous to represent a test of the hypothesis. Perhaps classmates meet our view of ourself because we "feed it to them" rather than the reverse. The failure to confirm the second part of the researchers' hypothesis suggests as much.

One study such as Cavior and Dokecki's, with its suspect definition and limited sampling, cannot alone invalidate the generalities of Mead's hypothesis. However, the limited variance accounted for by one's estimate of how one's peers see one as against how they in fact do (even on as mundane a measure as physical appearance) suggests that other factors take part in the construction of the self-concept. There are many influential theorists (Adler, 1956; Allport, 1960; Hartmann, 1951; Rogers, 1961; Sullivan, 1953; White, 1960) whose consensus argument is that some sort of idiosyncratic energy, not mere social feedback, is basic to a healthy self. The self is not only the "me," the passive object, but also the "I," the active subject. Mead does not in fact deny "I" and "me" aspects of the self; indeed he discusses them explicitly (1934). However the emphasis of his analysis is on the social process as it penetrates inward to the individual through the medium of language. The mind is thus primarily social. While Mead's view is dominated by a social-behavioral view of the self according to Tibbetts (1975, pp. 228–229), the "I" does have the potential to make some impact on society and constitutes the actions of the individual toward the attitudes of others.[4] While the self then has a dynamic aspect in addition to the social, its presumed source of energy seems vague in Mead, sometimes suggesting something akin to Freud's id (1934, p. 210), again containing hints of autonomy (1934, p. 197).

In the 50 years since Mead's theorizing, some theorists have reversed his emphasis by focusing more on the formal qualities of the ego[5] itself. Hartmann (1951), within the psychoanalytic tradition, argued that it is not necessary or even accurate to view all ego activities as a function of personality conflict, caught inevitably between the demands of society and id appetites. The mental functions of object mastery, or solving of logic problems, among others, are seen as essentially conflict-free tasks:

> Mental development is not solely a result of the struggle with drives, with love-objects, with the superego, and so on . . . memory, associations, and so on, are functions which cannot possibly be derived from the relationship of the ego to the drives or the love-objects; but rather are taken for granted in our conception of these relationships and their development [p. 371].

The autonomous aspects of the psyche are what may permit us a measure of freedom and give us the strength to resist cultural pressures and conformity demands potentially overwhelming to a more created, less creative self. It is our "self-esteem" as contrasted with "social esteem," to use Rogers' (1961) designations. While the psychopath may readily be viewed as overbalanced on the former, with his rapacious ego (cf. Frankenstein, 1959), it is nonetheless arguable as to whether he is as seriously crippled and out-of-phase as the Gough–Mead analysis would indicate. If Gough has drawn the correct thread to the psychopath from Mead, then the psychopath is in reality stupid:

> It is generally recognized that the specifically social expressions of intelligence, or the exercise of what is often called "social intelligence," depends upon the given individual's ability to take the roles of, or "put himself in the place of," the other

---

[4]The fact that Tibbetts (1975) and Katz (1963) come to such different views of Mead suggests ambiguity in his position, and probably also the difference in Mead's concept of behaviorism compared to more stringent views.

[5]Freud's ego seems roughly equivalent to self as "I."

individuals implicated with him in given social situations; and upon his consequent sensitivity to their attitudes toward himself and toward one another. These specifically social expressions of intelligence, of course, acquire unique significance in terms of our view that the whole nature of intelligence is social to the very core—that this putting of one's self in the places of others, this taking by one's self of their roles or attitudes, is not merely one of the various aspects or expressions of intelligence or of intelligent behavior, but is the very essence of its character [Mead, 1934, p. 141].

The view of the psychopath as deficient in intelligence hardly supports the usual clinical picture.

Saltzstein (1975) set out to observe how moral decisions might be influenced by role-taking training, obviously important for theories like Gough–Mead that make role or perspective-taking an essential ingredient in the making of appropriate moral decisions. American fourth, fifth, and sixth grade boys and girls responded to three moral dilemmas (in story form) originally created by Kohlberg. The experimental children were given role-taking training on two of four such stories. Training involved having the child answer questions from the respective points-of-view of, e.g., three main characters, in moral dilemmas bearing on trust and obligation. Reasoning at Kohlberg's developmental stages, which progress from self-serving to universalist levels of morality, served as dependent measures. A control group was also challenged to answer questions about the stories, but without the benefit of the experimental group's role coaching.

The results, based on 17 experimental and 23 control subjects, showed a general tendency for the trained children to show a higher level of moral reckoning than the controls that lasted over a 2-month period. Saltzstein felt these results were encouraging.

But only about one-half to two-thirds of the experimental children changed in the direction of higher-stage morality—as did one-quarter to one-third of the untutored control children. Most important for the issue of morality as a function of role-taking was the researcher's attempt to demonstrate transfer to stories not coached. Here the results were equivocal, with one story showing significant transfer, and another not. Few of the subjects moved into stage three, which involved taking a "generalized perspective," not unlike Mead's "generalized other."[6]

Saltzstein also noted how small were the changes which did occur—generally substantially less than one Kohlberg stage. He hopes to increase changes with improved role-taking practice. He acknowledged that role-taking may be necessary but not sufficient to moral progress.

[6] Kohlberg's developmental view of moral reasoning is not founded on the premise that morality is predominantly an internalization of social teachings (Hogan, 1975).

His final comment may serve as a gentle reminder to those who might over-generalize the social aspect of self:

> If the cognitive–developmental point of view is proved correct, the principle will again be affirmed that change in thought requires the active participation of the person to be changed. In the end no one can change you fundamentally but yourself [1975, p. 11].

A BEHAVIORISTIC EXPLANATION

As already noted, behaviorists have generally found the Gough–Mead formulation congenial, very likely because of the emphasis on the social origins of those qualities that appear to make the person distinctly human. As Mead told it, we can feel for others because we can take their point of view; we can empathize. Further, Mead designated himself a social behaviorist, although he distinguished himself from colleague John Watson's behaviorism regarding the nature of thought (Mead, 1934), since he did not reflexly avoid discussing symbols or intentions (Tibbetts, 1975).

But the paradox for a behavioral solution to the problem of the nature of psychopathy impertinently arises: How does this person known as a psychopath, who suffers a basic failure of empathy, manage to be so finely tuned to the needs of others that he can manipulate them "like a puppet on a string?" Indeed the entire *raison d'être* of certain psychopaths seems predicated on reading the wishes, wills, weaknesses of others, then dangling the appropriate variety of carrot until the other succumbs. Is a capacity for at least a certain kind of empathy, feeling the other's potential embarrassment to exposure in a con game, for example, not essential to this manipulation? As noted, some enthusiasts for the most superficial variety of role theory easily dismiss the psychopath as a poor player of roles. The inappropriateness of this is obvious when we think of how very central role playing is in the life of the successful con artist or psychopath. What these people must mean is something much deeper than "role" as we are accustomed to think of it in talking about the role of father, the work role, the role of church-goer. This brings us back to Mead's analysis. As we saw, his way of conceiving of roles was not the relatively superficial way they are often treated by encounter group leaders or psychodramatists, for example. Ullmann and Krasner have not been so blindly naive as to flatly label the psychopath an inept role player. They acknowledge that the psychopath is even more skilled than the average person in influencing others to reinforce him; still he is judged a failure as a complete person. They explain the paradox in the following terms:

> Other people do not become effective secondary reinforcing stimuli for this individual. This is important because the vast majority of actions by others that are typically reinforcing are acquired or secondary reinforcing stimuli. The person called a psychopath is, if anything, more skilled than average in emitting behavior that will influence others to act in a manner that is explicitly reinforcing. He is able to sell himself to others, and the payment they make by not punishing him or by giving him a good job is indeed reinforcing. Other people, then, seem to serve as secondary reinforcing stimuli. The distinction here is between the seducer and the genuine lover. The psychopath may indeed sell himself well and apparently be influenced (i.e., reinforced in the sense that his behavior is altered) by the extrinsic reinforcement of the other person's compliance. In fact, he may be even more effective as salesman or seducer than the average person because he is not paying attention to the other person's welfare: he is less likely to avoid lying to the other person and to worry about the ultimate aversive consequences for the other person [1969, p. 455].

Elsewhere in their otherwise careful discussion, these authors flatly state that the psychopath is a poor player of social roles (p. 454), but we can ignore this casual lapse and examine the above quotation, which represents their most careful attempt to explain the psychopath as a good–poor role player. As I read the above quotation, the authors are saying that other people become secondary reinforcers for the psychopath, but in only a superficial, not genuine fashion. As example they suggest to us a seducer–genuine lover distinction. A casual reading suggests that there is little wrong with this distinction; the reader grasps it readily from his own experience repertoire. But from the ostensibly behavioral analysis that Ullmann and Krasner propose for abnormality in general and the psychopath in particular, what does this distinction tell us? How can one *behaviorally distinguish* the lover from the seducer? We might agree that in some way the former seems more genuine, more committed, more empathic. But then we are thrown back to the question of what genuineness, or commitment, or empathy means behaviorally. Does one count the number of sexual couplings in deciding who is the genuine lover and who the seducer? Who—layman or professional—has not been at least once duped by a "psychopath" who gave every indication of being a "genuine lover, warm and true?"

Perhaps the whole notion of playing a role is semantically unfortunate. Depth of feeling for others does not seem wholly congenial with such a locution.

Hendrick (1977) has underscored the Meadian distinction between *role playing* and *role taking*. The former is common to dramatic performances or to enacting the role of family member. Role taking involves comparing one's own cognitions with the cognitions of others and then formulating adaptive behavior. The process is illustrated in conversation, according to Hendrick, where reaction to the thoughts, feelings, and expectancies of the other guides the conversation. But this mutual "perspective-taking" (p. 468), with its strong cognitive element, would seem to present no special problem for the psychopath. I shall argue later that in a culture with the appropriate prerequisites the psychopath is ideally suited to making the cognitively appropriate responses.

A concept such as "genuine core self" or the "authentic being" of Rogers (1961), or Maslow (1962), Jasper's transcendent Being, even Freud's "genital character" all seem more amenable constructs than secondary reinforcement when distinctions such as "depth of response" become the issue. But the problem is more than simply semantic; we are talking about two fundamentally different metatheories regarding how the person is viewed and judged. A behavioral analysis simply fails when employed to address such admitted subtleties.

I have remarked elsewhere (1973) that although the psychopath's empathic skills may indeed be impaired when compared with some normative average for this capacity, it is only an assumption to believe so. I do not know that such a hypothesis has been meaningfully tested since that writing.[7] Empathy is a tricky if not impossible notion to get an empirical fix on (cf. Hunsdahl, 1967; Luchins, 1957), and how it may or may fail to be integrated into the personality remains equally contentious.

Truax (1966) has built an "Accurate Empathy Scale" to assess the quality of empathy among therapists in responding to statements made by clients during therapy sessions. For Truax, empathy is sensitivity to the feelings of the client, and the verbal ability to communicate this to the client in tune with the latter's feelings. Unfortunately, in one study scale scores correlated highly with both therapist warmth and with the semantic differential dimension, "good–bad," suggesting the scale may be measuring some global "good quality" (Rappaport & Chinsky, 1972). Perhaps worse, in several studies there were significant correlations between Accurate Empathy and number of words spoken by the therapist. Wenegrat (1976) examined responses of client-centered therapy tape segments used for the training of Accurate Empathy Raters. Of 17 measures employed, an overall Accurate Empathy rating correlated highest with therapist assertiveness in discussing client emotions. Positive Accurate Empathy correlates such as number of words spoken by therapist, do not seem to tap any empathic subtlety beyond

---

[7]Guterman (1970) points to an interesting research area in suggesting that accurate person perception may have little to do with empathy. He remarked also that high Mach V scorers (Christie & Geis, 1970) were good judges of others.

the reach of a manipulative individual. Rappaport and Chinsky also noted that therapist's self-ratings are frequently unrelated to client perceptions regarding empathy, and that Carkhuff and Burstein (1970) have argued that clients cannot be trusted to make such judgments, only "other high-level empathizers." One is not made more comfortable concerning the role of the counselor by Abramson's (1973) finding that graduate students enrolled in a counseling practicuum scored significantly higher on the "Machiavellian Tactics" items from the "Mach V" test (see Chapter 6) than did other advanced psychology students.

SUMMARY

Role theory explanations of what psychopathy constitutes have an intuitive appeal, and appear satisfactory as one way of conceptualizing the seeming inhumanity of psychopathic behavior. Role playing has a behavioral ring and has proven attractive to partisans of behaviorism. However "role" as Mead and other sociological role theorists use the term is much more complex and surplus in meaning than could be expected to gladden the heart of a rigorous behaviorist. One enters the land of empathy, depth of feeling, and "good faith," and whereas these may all be prefaced by concern for one's fellows, they wrench the notion of role sharply out of its frequently defined track of "acting as if" one were doctor, lawyer, or Indian chief. The psychopath is master at this latter aspect of role assumption, and therefore an element of paradox is presented. This issue does not seem to be alleviated or illuminated by casting it in terms of genuine and superficial reinforcers, or even role playing/role taking, not least because of the subtleties, even ambiguities, in roles seen as imaginative processes.

Research based on behavior modeling techniques such as Saltzstein's exemplifies this more mundane view of roles, where children are only verbally engaged to decide on the morality of characters in abstract stories. It would be interesting to see how children (also controlled for the important variable of IQ) showing other indications of prepsychopathic status would handle such morality training. There is nothing in the diagnosis of psychopathy of clinical specialists like Cleckley to suspect that such children would have any difficulty exhibiting "moral" responses. The psychopath does, supposedly, "know the words if not the music" (Cleckley, 1964).[8]

---

[8] However, a recent study (Campagna & Harter, 1975) indicated that male children (ages 10–13) defined as psychopathic on a behavior (acting out) checklist showed less moral maturity to Kohlberg stories than did a control group of children. The effect persisted, although substantially weaker, when Wechsler Verbal IQ was partialled out.

Even Mead's subtle conception of role, as employed to explain formation of the self-concept, seems narrow and lopsided. While Mead himself gave the "I" some power in relation to the "me," his analysis of society against the self clearly gave major power to the latter. Gough's widely quoted analysis of psychopathy takes exclusively this perspective and suffers accordingly when one considers not only Mead's theory, but other perspectives of the self as seen in the writings of Allport, Adler, White, and others. I am not aware that Mead himself ever made direct reference to the psychopath, so it is understandable, if distorting, that Gough took from Mead that which supported what he saw as the major failing of the psychopath.

The psychopath may have quite a strong "I" or ego. At the same time he or she does not seem deficient in social intelligence by any criteria I have seen. Mead wrote that intelligence is more than the putting of one's self in the places of others and taking their roles and attitudes toward oneself and one another. It is also taking the attitude of society toward "the various phases or aspects of the common social undertakings in which, as members of an organized society or social group, they are all engaged . . . [1934, pp. 154–155]." In a society where the significant others are frequently engaged in exploiting people for their own gain, the psychopath would seem to be the very essence of social intelligence. In this regard Berg (1974), employing a U. S. sample, found a significantly smaller real–ideal self discrepancy among psychopathic than among neurotic criminal offenders, even while there were no significant differences in the ideal selves projected by the two groups. The psychopathic offenders described themselves as "daring, adventurous, clear-thinking, outspoken, warm-hearted and unselfish [1974, p. 622]."

5
Cleckley and the Psychopath

Hervey Cleckley may be as prominent for his case study of Eve and her three faces as he is for successive editions of *The Mask of Sanity*, but with respect to impact on theory in its subject matter realm, the latter work has clearly surpassed the former. That subject matter realm is psychopathy, and Cleckley has reached a very wide audience with his writing about this syndrome since his first edition in 1941. Even non-professionals quote him extensively (cf. Harrington, 1974), and he is perhaps *the* recognized expert in the AngloAmerican literature. Among his emphases have been the focusing of attention on the potential psychopathology in the otherwise only behaviorally aberrant psychopath's make up, as well as the freeing of various of the criminally delinquent from the opprobrium of the label "psychopath." He has accomplished this latter by showing the psychopathic animal in everyday garb as businessman, lawyer, physician, etc., which has substantially contributed to a broader view of the phenomenon. At the same time he has argued for a difference in feeling tone between a run-of-the-mill delinquent and a classic psychopath.

Many of the things which the psychopath does are typical of the delinquent but seem to constitute only a part of his life expression, perhaps a relatively small part.

> . . . Although anxiety, remorse, shame, and other consciously painful subjective
> responses to undesirable consequences are deficient in both as compared with the
> normal, this callousness or apathy is far deeper in the psychopath. The deficiency is
> also far more successfully masked [1976, p. 268].

Not least, Cleckley has provided the basic criterial signs (see Chapter 2) to help the diagnosticians among us make less sweeping, waste-basket inclusions of every case that crosses social boundaries and fits none of our other diagnostic pigeonholes.

PSYCHOPATHY OR LIBERATED SEXUALITY?

Where Cleckley's fascinating and frequently delightful treatise runs into trouble, in my opinion, is in the realm of judgments defining specific behaviors as psychopathic. Women with difficulties come off particularly poorly when their sexual behavior undergoes his scrutiny:

> Although the excitement of physical relations seemed to have been genuine and full
> vaginal orgasm occurred and left her without the feeling that anything might be
> lacking, the experiences reported impressed the examiner, in some important re-
> spects, as relatively shallow. . . . She was cognizant of the old analogy between getting
> the first olive out of a bottle and getting the first kiss and its even greater applicability
> to what she had offered without even initial delay or any impediment whatsoever.
> . . . No evidence emerged of an appreciable sense of shame on her part or of an un-
> easiness about meeting unflattering attitudes and appraisals that might develop
> toward a girl who lets herself be taken so readily. . . . Completion of the sexual act
> was not followed by remorse or self incrimination. Relieved and pleased, she had no
> wish for any sort of personal closeness or intimacy with her companion but, on the
> other hand, she did not feel strong revulsion [1976, pp. 273–274].

Although this case is labeled a "circumscribed behavior disorder," Cleckley later judged her sexual activity "entirely typical of what we find in the true psychopath [1976, p. 285]."

But look again at the adjectives describing the sexual experiences of this unnamed lady in her middle twenties: "genuine and full vaginal orgasm," "no feeling of anything lacking," "no feeling of remorse," "relieved and pleased." Such description of a male's subjective ex-periences of sexuality would almost invariably be looked on by clini-cians as well integrated and quite psychologically healthy. Have they not a generally positive sound? Where are objective indications of shallowness?

The same young woman, observed Cleckley, enjoyed watching, from a distance as it were, a suitor go through various "rituals of deception so common and sometimes rather elaborate, which the predatory male uses to get his way with the ladies [1976, p. 275]." This reportedly made the patient feel "one up" for seeing through the man with whom she had every intention of cooperating anyway, and let no hate or contempt emerge in her behavior.

In an existential sense the girl's attitude toward the situation might be judged quite appropriate. This reportedly intelligent and successful woman's sexual experiences, rather than validating her pathology, point up instead the dishonesty in our conventional rating–dating system, and the inherent bad faith (*mauvaise foi,* Sartre, 1956) in the roles traditionally prescribed for men and women of Western habit. In the example here, she is supposed to tell a lie with her body, to feign disinterest, to reject what she would rather accept—in short to manipulate like a psychopath toward some nebulous goal of male respect. Cleckley views the poor girl as pathetically inappropriate because she did not do this: "It had not occurred to her that this would be regarded by most as an almost fantastically inaccurate way of scoring in such a contest, since the adversary never failed to gain all his ends [1976, p. 275]."

The attitude of the author regarding relations between the sexes is tipped off by the "contest-scoring" analogy and the mention of how most would score the game, as if how it were regarded by "most" in the United States in the 1950s was the definitive point in judging her psychological health. In a recent essay on self-esteem and human equality, Belaief characterizes American society as corresponding ontogenetically to the juvenile period with regard to needs, values, and institutions. These values base mother love, for example, on performance-oriented stress. A society so oriented must eschew human equality in favor of competition, she argues

> Unless the relation has some practical purpose which fits the motivation of en-
> lightened self-interest, the juvenile schema cannot comprehend its meaning. It is
> almost as if such actions were invisible to the larger society. For example, many are
> deeply convinced that equality in sex, that is a reciprocity and sharing of pleasure, is
> somehow impossible, so that sexual relationships are misperceived as an unequal
> exploitive situation [Belaief, 1976, pp. 34–35].

It seems clear that the young lady did not behave exploitatively in this example chosen by Cleckley, and she is condemned for not doing so.

While self-contempt may have been functioning at some level of the girl's motive hierarchy, Cleckley, with guileless honesty from our present perspective, reported that she did not, through this ritual, come to dislike or despise her eventual partner. Nor did she find it necessary to indicate that she saw through his activity, or even to thwart him—

responses we might expect from a truly hostile manipulator on the borderline of psychopathy. Quite the contrary, might there not be something of the psychopath in *males* who proceed in this way with a companion? Is their behavior less alienated from their being in its patent, smug exploitation, even if this is widely accepted, indeed culturally approved? It is a very prosaic, enculturated viewpoint that turns this honest, sexually nonexploitative woman into a pathological loser and latent hater of men on the evidence given. Cleckley traced the patient's behavior to disappointment in a homosexual affair with an older woman—a deeply satisfying relation, we are told, broken off by the latter rather abruptly, if legitimately, through a necessary move to another city. He concluded that the girl had been "throwing herself away" on men because she had been thrown away by her female lover.

Her early history was also judged to contribute to her difficulties. As a young girl she felt that boys and men had all the advantages simply as a sexual birthright. Because she was also punished arbitrarily by her father, Cleckley finds fertile grounds for her strange behavior:

> Marriage was very strongly rejected as an ambition. Reactions to her mother and to her father apparently combined in this negative force and contributed to a distorted response to this major feminine role. She examined again and felt again the effects upon her of her older brother. It was he for whom money had to be saved so that he could go to medical school. She recalled that at first she had been very fond of him and proud of him. As she continued to reorient herself to what had appeared to be preference on the parents' part for his ambitions, while deprivations were demanded of her so that he could attain the independence of being a physician, she became better able to see these things in the general context of her life [1976, pp. 282–283].

Cleckley observed that her attitudes eventually righted themselves through psychotherapy. This was seen in her admission that male and female sex organs

> get better sensual results than anything possible with two female bodies, which are not anatomically equippped for such a feat [1976, p. 283].
>
> [Still] it was less difficult for her to give up her sexual promiscuity than to alter her attitudes toward marriage [1976, p. 300].

Cleckley's reasons for deciding this girl's psychopathic sexuality was not definitive in making her a true psychopath were adumbrated earlier, e.g., her successful work history. While her sexual relations and orientation were "bizarre," on his analysis, he held out hope for her because

> Not only was this young lady consistently successful and purposive in her work and in all other social relations, but her emotional attitudes and responses in almost every

situation except those centering about sexual aims were normal and adequate [1976, p. 285].

While we do not learn from this history if the girl settled down to home, husband, and children like a good *Hausfrau*, psychotherapy seems to have put her on the "right" track.

THE FAILURE OF TREATMENT

It would indeed be interesting to know the eventual fate of this young lady, now a middle-aged woman facing the late 1970s. Might she have cause to regret those alterations in the direction of the happy, integrated heterosexual American woman, or were these changes only superficial and designed to please her therapist? Perhaps we should hope for the latter, since times are altering sexual role expectations and maybe as an intelligent person she finds herself once again out of step, thanks to her therapeutic experiences. Indeed, she may require a therapist to reaffirm these trends perhaps now to be judged healthy; she may simply have been a woman born ahead of her time. Such speculation is more than intellectual gamesmanship on my part. Should a therapist bend the psyche of such persons into time-bound cultural roles?[1] It has become painfully clear that treatment for the psychopath that focuses on altering the individual presents a task beside which cleaning the Augean stable looms simple. And Cleckley himself is perhaps the first to ackowledge this, although back in 1955 he was still guardedly optimistic about potential treatment modalities:

> Mangun reports encouraging results when adequate institutional control can be obtained and consistent nonpunitive therapeutic discipline applied in addition to other psychotherapeutic methods. Woolley also expresses hopefulness about such measures. As matters now stand, it is hardly accurate to say that treatment of psychopaths has been given a reasonable trial. Perhaps it is an exaggeration to say there has been a trial at all with most of these patients [1955, p. 534].[2]

He also looked with some favor on one of the more coercive change measures:

> Some years ago a few observers reported good results from prefrontal lobotomy in case of behavior disorder apparently similar to those we are discussing. . . . More

[1] I do not intend this as an attack on Cleckley; it is meant as a general query for all of us as therapists. We are all more or less guilty of this, perhaps unavoidably. We were even more guilty of it in the two decades preceding this one.
[2] This and subsequent quotations cited to Cleckley, 1955 are reprinted by permission of The C. V. Mosby Co. from Cleckley, Hervey, *The Mask of Sanity*, ed. 3, St. Louis, 1955.

recently Darling and Sanddal have studied the effects of transorbital lobotomy in 18 psychopaths, most of them extremely severe cases. In all but one remarkably encouraging results were observed. More than one-half of these patients are reported as leading well-adjusted lives in the community, some of them for more than a year [1955, p. 536].

Certainly since the time of this quotation, it has become clear that lobotomies may curtail some undesirable behaviors, such as aggressive attacks, but the adjacent desirable behaviors also adversely affected, e.g., social responsibility, make this treatment questionable in the extreme. Even when pessimistic, for example regarding his own lack of treatment success with these cases, Cleckley favored forced hospitalization and restraint so that therapeutic measures could be instituted. Nine years later he still favored institutional commitment (he has not been alone in this belief; see McCord & McCord, 1964) and lamented the psychopath's immunity from legal control (1964, p. 474). Even while recognizing the danger to civil liberty, he argued that confinement might be the preferred condition:

Some practical help might be afforded in controlling the sociopath by the general application of laws designed to increase progressively the penalty and term of confinement for those who repeatedly demonstrate by antisocial acts that they have not learned through experience and that they are still dangerous to the community [1964, p. 475].[3]

His optimism, guarded though it was in 1955, later appeared seriously dampened:

For a while I had hoped that long-term treatment might be more effective if the patient could be induced voluntarily or constrained by commitment procedures to remain with the therapist for enough time to give his methods a thorough and adequate trial. I am no longer as hopeful that any methods available today would be successful with typical sociopaths. I have now, after more than two decades, had the opportunity to observe a considerable number of patients who, through commitment or the threat of losing their probation status or by other means, were kept under treatment not only for many months but for years. The therapeutic failure in all such patients observed leads me to feel that we do not at present have any kind of psychotherapy that can be relied upon to change the psychopath fundamentally. Nor do I believe that any other method of psychiatric treatment has shown promise of solving the problem. Physical methods of therapy including electric shock have been attempted. Prefrontal lobotomy, topectomy, and transorbital lobotomy have been used in a few patients with severe disorder. Some encouragement was expressed by a few observers about the effects of these measures, but apparently they have not proved to be a real solution of the problem [1964, pp. 477–478; 1976, p. 439].

[3]This and subsequent quotations cited to Cleckley, 1964 are reprinted by permission of The C. V. Mosby Co. from Cleckley, Hervey, *The Mask of Sanity*, ed. 4, St. Louis, 1964.

Why these conspicuous treatment failures? Cleckley swings from strict institutional commitment to lobectomy for signals of success and admits discouragement with the failures. Granting the impressive failures of numerous treatment modalities, confinement serves little more than a punitive function. The psychopath as Cleckley views him represents a usually mild, capricious threat to society, compared to the damage wreaked by organized crime, for example, so protection cannot be a major rationale for what would amount to jailing.[4] Cleckley seems to have backed into a cul-de-sac: Treatment has been a failure and confinement is superfluous. The only escape route lies in labeling the psychopath mentally ill, which would then afford the familiar channels of official complaint, intake, and treatment.

A "MASK OF SANITY"

Cleckley judges psychopathy to be a unique breed of mental illness. If a successful treatment modality were to be discovered, those diagnosed as psychopaths would still require guidance and restraint when returned to the community.[5] There are several problems with this conception. First, psychiatric diagnosis itself is under heavy attack because of the problem of defining cases at the border regions of various syndromes, with resulting conceptual confusion. The problem of distinguishing a neurotic depressive from a psychotic depressive is one such example. And the momentum of criticism since the Hollingshead and Redlich study (1958) showing correlations between social class and diagnosis, plus Szasz's disenchantment (1960) has accelerated rather than diminished (cf. Albee, 1970). Second, what criteria are there for labeling the psychopath mentally ill? Does he show the hallucinations of the hebephrenic? No. The paralyzing anxieties of the obsessive-compulsive? No. The unstoppable energy of the manic? No. Depression? No. And so on ad nauseum.

If there are no specific intrapsychic difficulties plaguing those labeled psychopaths, as Karpman (1948) also specifically argued, where do we

---

[4]In spite of the word "danger" in the above quote the weight of Cleckley's argument is that the psychopath is more a nuisance threat (cf. 1976, p. 437). The McCords, defining the psychopath more broadly, take his potential for danger much more seriously (cf. 1956, p. 36).

[5]Briefly, he sees the problem as one of "semantic dementia" where "the sufferer knows the words, but not the tune." This formulation parallels that of Gough–Mead in that something on the surface, i.e., the words, is out of joint with a deeper mechanism, i.e., subjective meaning.

look for etiological factors in this behavior? Much of the physiological research postdates Cleckley's main publication, and an absence of a discussion of it there is not surprising.[6] More strangely, in the work under discussion, he never seriously broaches the potential role of the over-arching culture in the genesis of psychopathy.[7] In Cleckley's analysis, the society is treated essentially as a constant and it is the individual who represents variance. Not once does he take the logical step—having himself provided the criteria and examples for distinguishing the psychopath from cases of clear intrapsychic conflict—of looking at the social world in which the psychopath carries out his robust activities. Cleckley's case studies, while absorbing, are first of all narrowly American, so that there is no hint of the generality, incidence, treatment, or other specifics of this problem as it is manifested in other cultures.[8] This fact may be at the root of his more significant failure to examine critically the modes and mores of that one society with which he is concerned. Might not, for example, failure of a person to produce feelings in tune with responses have cultural determinants? It is as if the American culture were taken as representative of the world at large, therefore leaving no other cultural standpoint from which to judge the behaviors presented.

This is not to say that the psychopath is of necessity free of intrapsychic conflict and therefore invariably the picture of psychological health. In any society we might expect individuals to flaunt the prevailing norms for idiosyncratic reasons—reasons convincingly demonstrated in numerous psychiatric treatises and supported by reams of psychological research. I do want to suggest that in many cases intrapsychic conflict is a small part of the variance that constitutes psychopathic problems, and we ignore cultural variables only at great peril to better understanding such behavior. Distinguishing the family circle as cultural input from the modes and mores of the over-arching culture is also of primary importance here. The family is of course itself a product of the larger culture and will reflect significant elements of the broader social fabric in its dynamic interactions. And childrearing modes have certainly not been ignored by theorists concerned with psychopathy (Buss, 1966; Frankenstein, 1959; McCord & McCord, 1964; White, 1964). Nonetheless individual families may be light years away

[6] There are brief allusions to Hare's discussion of EEG findings in Cleckley's fifth edition (1976).

[7] Still Cleckley is not alone guilty of this kind of unconscious ethnocentrism; it pervades, e.g., American social psychology (cf. Moscovici, 1972).

[8] He, like nearly all theorists and researchers on this topic, mentions the family and its various constellations in producing psychopathic persons, but the analysis stops there.

from modal personality (Inkeles & Levinson, 1969) representations, from "national character training." The latter is the main focus of our present interest, as it stretches out from mass media forms to mold us all in uniform direction.

PSYCHOPATHY AND MYTHS OF A CULTURE

The American culture is heavily invested in the ideal of individual achievement and accumulation of material wealth as a sign of God's favor (Weber, 1930, first published 1904; Tawney, 1947). Our enduring hero is the man who can propel himself out of the mass and battle to the top of the socioeconomic ladder. And our advice to the ladies is marry well because "diamonds are a girl's best friend." Although they never approximated reality, Horatio Alger heroes, whose hard work, thrift, and honesty inevitably brought success, conditioned the hopes and dreams of several generations of immigrants. Seeing that the streets of America were not in fact paved with gold, they set out to repave them through hard work and long hours: The good life awaited the diligent. This ideal, monotonously repeated in mass art forms through the period of World War II, has since given way to a new ethos where heroes must show strong interpersonal skills and a knowledge of how to get the most out of others, presumably for their own benefit: It is the era of the manager. An example from the highest political echelons is instructive. Political writers found Lyndon Johnson's well-known ability to *get his way* "in the cloakrooms of Congress" a compelling reason for preferring Johnson's Democratic presidential candidacy to John Kennedy's.

American men of the cloth changed with the times as well, and indeed may have helped to create them. Norman Vincent Peale and Billy Graham do not breathe hell-fire and damnation at disbelievers, but patience and faith so that the fruits of the earth shall be yours, as they have indeed been theirs. In the post-war domination of the psyche by moving visual forms (cf. McLuhan & Fiore, 1967), the form of the image looms more important than its substance. Whether initially true or false, it has become a solidly ingrained bit of folklore that Kennedy defeated Richard Nixon in the narrow presidential voting of 1960 because Nixon looked so tense and drawn, i.e., his make-up on camera was inferior to that of Kennedy.[9]

It is in America that the saying "I don't care what you say about me as

---

[9] The young and relatively unknown Kennedy obtained the party candidacy not least because he was more attractive personally than was Johnson—and had a prettier wife.

long as you spell my name right," has been raised to the level of a philosophical axiom—a slogan to live by. Barroom arguments over the merit of a record or book become routinely (and triumphantly) settled with a statement such as "It must be good, it sold a million!"[10] "Madison Avenue" has become a Western World synonym for slick presentation of a product; this expanded in the 1960s from the product as cigarette or soapflake to the person as product—film star, political hopeful, and even "star" lawyer and physician. The image industry has made television the prime force in major political campaigns well calculated to dazzle the consumer with the visual stimulus, rather than concentrating on the message. The groundwork facilitating this magic circus will be explored in some depth further along. Suffice it here to say that the psychopath may not be mad when he shows exaggerated skills in the afore-mentioned directions. Remember that the following are prominent among the psychopath's basic characteristics (Cleckley, 1964): (a) superficial charm and good intelligence; (b) lack of remorse or shame; (c) untruthfulness and insincerity; and (d) pathologic egocentricity and incapacity for love. When such "capacities" are thrown into a pot bubbling with high achievement motivation (cf. McClelland's fascinating research, 1961, 1969), image-making, and respect for those persons possessing the most market value (Fromm, 1955), it is not suprising if the result is a deadly witch's brew belching forth like some chemist's nightmare, showering over, and thereby coloring, the values of those standing by.

Such a set of values forms a tailor-made arena for psychopathic acting out. A classic example of a psychopathic success story is the case of Ferdinand Waldo Demara, Jr. Demara was a nobody who, like many Americans in those circumstances, wanted to be somebody. Showing even less constraint than most of us, he took the quickest route: With consummate gall he impersonated any role that could measure up to his ego. Thus he "became" politician, naval officer, and psychologist. In the latter guise, which he assumed after "suiciding" his way out of the navy, he taught, among other courses at a small Canadian college, Abnormal Psychology! In his convoluted career he next entered (with forged papers) the Royal Canadian Navy as a medical officer. Forced by the circumstance of the Korean War into performing combat surgery

---

[10]The "serious" publishing business is also no longer exempt from this philosophy. In a discussion with a senior editor from a highly respected publishing house, a manuscript by a man whose fame rested on exercise classes conducted over television was pointed out to me. The book concerned the man's personal experiences rather than his work. The editor was certain the book would earn money for all parties simply because of the author's notoriety—and thus would be published.

(although he had never even been witness to an operation), Demara performed well, so well in fact that the subsequent publicity was his undoing. He became so famous that he could no longer impersonate others without being recognized himself!

Repeatedly unmasked, did our man suffer degradation and long incarceration for these illegal acts? On the contrary, he became the focus of a book and the hero of a film (only Hollywood could be so rigidly image-conscious as to have kept him from playing himself), and on last report was alive and well in "a small northwestern community" serving, with the congregation's full knowledge of his past, as a minister of God (Coleman, 1972). Demara's behavior could stand as a model for all budding and actual American psychopaths: Think big enough and the world can be yours—at least part of this one. Imagine what moral lessons he is able to interpret to a sinning congregation.

Cleckley and others of us who overlook broad cultural forces in producing personality configurations must seem especially naive to the really clever psychopath exposed to their theories. With his good intelligence it must be patently obvious to the psychopath that it is the hospital or "therapeutic community," with its lock-step demands on issues of petty morality, that is the "sick" environment rather than being a microcosm of reality to which he ought to "shape up." Outside are millionaire pop stars, business heroes like Bernard Kornfeld, and men like former President Nixon and his team, who represent the reality that counts. That's where it really happens—the cool world, where even famous novelists write paeons to the "hip" (Mailer, 1957). Why not play along with the funny institution rules if it will ingratiate the stupid authorities and permit one to get back where the world is waiting for the really big operator?

In a work marred by examples of clearly psychotic behavior lumped indiscriminately with some good psychopathic examples (see Chapter 9), writer Alan Harrington (1974) does provide one excellent illustration of professional blindness—the confrontation of honest, well-meaning authority with an arch-cynic psychopath. The case involved a part-time automobile salesman, part-time rowdy, who was a regular customer on the police blotter and now and again turned up at the local mental hospital. The story itself was told to Harrington by a policeman who knew the case.

A psychiatrist who got himself assigned as "Ron's" therapist when he was on community parole decided Ron needed a friend who loved and was loyal to him so that he might develop a sense of trust in his fellow man. Thus our therapist "Dr. Ames" decided to become a social buddy of the man-about-town. Included in the therapeutic strategy of "getting to know" Ron were mutual "confessions" during which the doctor admitted his weaknesses and fears in exchange for like admissions from Ron. "I made up all kinds of sad stories about when I was a kid," Ron later reported. As might be expected, Ron's reaction to this promising friendship was extremely positive and he soon began taking his therapist to various poolrooms and bowling establishments and on all-night drinking sprees, where Ames' physical ineptness at games of skill and mild intake capacity made him the joke of Ron and his gang. Meanwhile, from his job as car salesman, Ron forced a small sports car on the doctor for his family of five. When Ames at first balked, Ron convinced him that it would permit him and his wife to feel "young again." We might already wonder who was therapist and who patient.

Ron thoroughly enjoyed both the accelerating discomfort and ready pocketbook of "Little Doc" as their relationship ripened. If this was what therapy was all about, he was all for it! Little Doc's wife was not all for it, however, and when Ron began calling from barrooms at two or three a.m. insisting his friend and therapist was needed, her enthusiasm declined even further, especially because her husband dutifully roused himself and joined his patient. This pace and ludicrous situation couldn't go on indefinitely, with Ron's early hour need for his friend seemingly increasing and Doc's family life steadily deteriorating. In inventorying his therapist's weaknesses, Ron noted that Ames was terrified of physical violence. He began playing on this—for the sheer fun of it, we are told, during therapy sessions. He would suddenly grip the doctor's wrist or shoulder and stare at him unspeaking. Doc then transferred therapy from his office to the hospital (to win back a bit of authority, one presumes). Ron simply began skipping appointments on a variable reinforcement schedule to keep his therapist on his toes. The doctor gave up at this point and was willing to declare Ron competent just to get rid of him—however, Ron refused! The upshot, Harrington tells us, was that Doc had "some kind of breakdown," and one day quietly left town not to return. Ron's friendship was a bigger burden than the doctor's job and local social position could counterbalance, and he sacrificed the latter to escape the former.

I judge that neither Cleckley, nor you, nor I would have fallen victim to the clever and even vicious manipulations of our operator Ron,[11] but I mention the case here simply to pose once again the question: Who is the more realistic citizen of our culture? Is it he who imposes these treatment extremes—from lockup to well-meaning (if ludicrous)

---

[11] Although Cleckley has written that when he is found lending funds to a patient, his staff automatically diagnoses "psychopath."

"friendship," or is it the psychopath who plays the game until he once again returns to society?

A pessimistic picture of psychopathy?—perhaps, but I choose to call it a realistic one that does not pretend that the solution lies in "socializing" the psychopath. With respect to the dominant, if sometimes covert, themes in his society, he is, if anything, oversocialized. We have evolved a social order for which the psychopath is admirably fitted.

6

Psychopathy:
Qualitative or Quantitative Entity?

In Chapter 1 varying historical viewpoints contributing to the designation of psychopath were discussed. These were compared from the perspective of the reigning social theories of the day, and from attitudes manifested toward such issues as moral turpitude, mental illness, and legal responsibility. The psychopath was viewed in the main as a deviate marked by whatever definition of pathology was prevalent at that time or place. "Criminal deviate," "morally insane," and "socially disadvantaged" are terms that reflect these changing perspectives; the psychopath under each of these views stood apart from other deviant types, e.g., schizophrenics, and from the remainder of society.

SOME TYPOLOGICAL VIEWS

Views of psychopathy that seek specific underlying traits or genotypes for distinguishing those who show this behavior from those who do not are the clearest examples of typological theory. Eysenck's theory of criminality previously discussed is an example. In addressing biological bases of individual differences, Eysenck has noted that there is considerable response specificity in the reactions of the ANS. Thus he

came to his familiar distinction between the cortically inhibited extravert and the cortically excited introvert. Regarding differential reaction
of ANS subsystems he has written

> It has been found that this specific innovation is characteristic of a given person even
> though many different types of stimuli may be utilized, and it has been found that
> this response specificity is preserved over periods of time extending to several years
> at least [1965b, p. 384].

Typology of another, although not necessarily unrelated sort, is displayed typically in psychiatric diagnosis. Here the displayer of symptoms, or "disease victim," is classified to a category where his or her
type is matched against an ideal or "classic" type. Cleckley's view of the
psychopath as not only a problem for society but also as a case of
derangement comes under this designation. The psychopath is judged a
special case requiring intensive treatment and extraordinary measures.
Cleckley's listed criteria (see Chapter 2) for diagnosis of psychopathy
are an effort to provide a symptom pattern that is at the same time
empirically relevant. McCord and McCord (1964), in spite of occasional
misgivings, also suggest a typological view. They see psychopathy as a
syndrome in which the character structure is judged defective. It is
probably no coincidence that they mention prominently the work of the
continental theorist, Aichorn, when they address the issue of treatment
for psychopathy. The program they favor seems to amount to efforts to
re-form basic character structure. In discussing interactional psychotherapy, Wolman has also enunciated a typological approach similar
to those of behavioral or Freudian advocates in its views regarding the
origin of psychopathy, i.e., broken home, parental rejection. Wolman
(1975), however, sees what he calls the "sink or swim," or "I must win
by hook or crook" (p. 151) attitude that he finds common among
rejected children as a form of narcissism corresponding to psychopathy
and believes "that the psychopathic personality is a clear-cut clinical
type and has the same five levels of severity as any other disorder [1975,
p. 151]."

Jablensky (1976) has noted that despite various dissatisfactions with
the diagnosis of psychopathy—often seen when diagnosers from different clinics or cultures make cross comparisons—most social scientists
still regard such diagnosing as clinically relevant. An influence on the
German psychiatric literature was Kant's notion of mental categories or
faculties, which formed the basis for positing individual differences.
An individual is thought to have a deviant mental constitution as a
result of an atypical distribution of cognitive faculties thereby providing the mold for deviant (from the norm) behavior. European emphasis

has continued to stress enduring, "mental constitution" bases for psychopathy and the personality disorders, as we saw with Schneider, where aberrant behavior plays a secondary role and there is no "antisocial personality" among his 10 types (Jablensky, 1976).

This emphasis on what seem to be the more stable aspects of psychopathy should be an aid in diagnosis. There are theoretical parsimony and practical treatment advantages possible to the extent that cases can be consistently fitted to the category. We have seen already however that the search for biological support, for example, has not been an altogether salutary one. In addition the question of the nature of types and the typing process continues to be debated.

Problems in Type Theory

Zubin has marked some of the problems inherent in diagnostic typing:

> Types thrive on the presence of discontinuities either in a given dimension or in the relationship between dimensions. Whether these discontinuities inhere in the behavior of the patient or in the behavior of the observer (his judgment of the presence of deviance) is still an open question. If the behavior of the patient is not separated by a discontinuity from the behavior of the rest of the population, but instead it is the observer who creates the discontinuity, the relativity of diagnosis in different cultural groups is a necessary result [1967, p. 377].

Philosopher/psychiatrist Jaspers has given a careful tripartite breakdown of the diagnosing of psychiatric concepts. The first involves psychiatric disorders where a clear somatic problem would be a central part of the syndrome: The example is an organic cerebral process. The second involves the search for totally psychic, internal events which would order phenotypic responses: His example is schizophrenia. The third involves extreme deviations from behavioral norms: The personality disorders are typical. Unfortunately for us, to the extent this scheme is reliable, psychopathic personalities, falling into group three, show little likelihood of being clearly specifiable, since Jaspers sees no clear-cut distinction between these cases and normal personalities:

> In Group III the only thing which is of value is an extensive analysis of the case, in its phenomenological, meaningful and causal aspects and a precise grasp on the personality, its reactions and life-history and its more weighty developments; but apart from some separation into a great number of type-groupings, diagnosis is an impossibility [quoted in Zubin, 1967, p. 380].

In European psychiatry the number of psychopathic types designated has risen as high as 16!

Zubin has expanded this essentially negative picture facing the diagnostician, adding

> The clinical approach depends primarily on the concept that specific entities of mental disorder exist and that the patients belonging to a given category have certain characteristics in common which are not shared by other groups. Thus, a certain discontinuity is postulated in the characteristics of the patients belonging to a given category. This discontinuity may refer to one characteristic, i.e., presence vs. absence of hallucinations, or it may refer to a discontinuity in the relationship between several characteristics, i.e., a combination or pattern of a certain degree of thinking disorder, a certain level of affect, and a certain degree of interpersonal contact as a syndrome of schizophrenia [1967, p. 398].

With respect to his earlier question as to whether possible discontinuities occur in the diagnosed person or in the judgment of the observer, Zubin added

> If it inheres in the patients, there is some hope of finding statistical methods for establishing the presence of nonoverlaping categories of disorder. However, if patient behavior is continuous with regard to the monovariate and multivariate distribution of their characteristics, we are faced with the problem of determining the threshold for discontinuity in the judgment of the observer. In the latter case our diagnostic procedures become highly dependent on the socio-cultural milieu of the patient and the schooling of the diagnostician [p. 398].

SOME QUANTITATIVE VIEWS

The idea that human behavior can be arranged along a continuum from normal to psychotic gained special prominence following Freud's familiar position that the normal differs from the neurotic or psychotic only in more successfully defending against impulses and in better adjustment to his society. This basic presupposition is implicit in the thinking of many theorists, and while the psychopath—because of his clinical picture of low manifest anxiety and good reality contact—is not easy to order on traditional symptom dimensions, he has nonetheless been so depicted by some theorists. Mowrer (1953) has, like Eysenck, seen the psychopath as having characteristics of the criminal and the neurotic. However, unlike Eysenck he proposes a normality–abnormality continuum along which the psychopath would occupy a position between the neurotic and the criminal, with the "normal" taking up a position to the left of the neurotic. He views the psychotic as merely an extreme neurotic.

Jaspers too, even if by default, offers a quantitative view of psychopathy, if not of abnormality in general. That is, the abnormal reactions of his Group III are only personality extremes which do not show any significant discontinuities from the normal. The diagnosis then is a question of the extent of the symptom, rather than its presence or absence.

Hare, whose physiological work we have encountered, has also expressed doubt that psychopathy can be treated as a unique clinical entity. At the same time he has pointed out some potential pitfalls in the dimensional or continuum approach:

> According to this view, psychopaths as such do not exist, although some individual may be considered more psychopathic than others if they occupy a more extreme position on some dimension that we choose to label "psychopathy." The difficulty here is that before we can really say that one person is more or less psychopathic than another, we need to know more about the makeup of the dimension. Assume, for example, that person A exhibits all of the characteristics that we feel are relevant to the dimension of psychopathy, and that person B exhibits only two-thirds of these characteristics. Who is the more psychopathic? If the dimension consists of the *number* of relevant characteristics, then person A would be considered more psychopathic than B. However, suppose that the characteristics exhibited by B, though fewer in number, are more severe than those shown by A. Who is the more psychopathic now? The problem becomes even more complicated if we assume that the defining features of psychopathy, or for that matter any other complex dimension of behavior, are not equally weighted—that is, that some are more important than others [1970, p. 12].

Hare goes on to point out that statistical techniques should permit combining number and severity of symptoms into a composite score. As previously noted, Zubin, too, hoped statistics might be diagnostically relevant, for example in quantifying the extent or degree of a symptom or pattern of symptoms.

Jablensky has argued that antisocial behavior must at least be separated from general social deviance, since behaviors associated with any mental illness may be socially deviant. Furthermore antisocial behavior is only one form of deviance. If the sociological (corresponding best to quantitative) view of personality disorder is contrasted with the medical/biological (qualitative) view, Jablensky's position is that:

> The sociological approach provides a complementary frame of reference that helps the more systematic study of social processes contributing to the manifestation, course, and outcome of mental disorders as well as the impact such disorders have on communities and societies [1976, p. 7].

While Jablensky views the personality disorders as quantitative, he sees their genesis in an abnormal personality structure.

Summary of the Quantitative Argument

There seems to be considerable agreement (cf. Jaspers, Gale, Hare, Zubin, Jablensky) that if reliable diagnostic entities outside the social–behavioral realm cannot be found, then a sociological approach must be sufficient. We have seen that up to this point (cf. Chapter 3) the evidence has given little to be optimistic about regarding the establishment of reliable genotypic, qualitative criteria. The viewpoint of the present analysis is that overarching cultural factors work back on the individual to discourage or enhance psychopathic-like behaviors. Certainly, individuals will be differentially affected by this cultural pressure dependent on nonbehavioral factors such as inherent physical energy, basic intelligence, etc. Persons with predispositions on nonbehavioral markers would simply be those most likely to "buckle" under the "call from the culture" and if other restraints were not present, to then win the epithet "psychopath." I prefer a quantitative model of psychopathy, because it incorporates the view that anyone in the culture is at least a potential victim. To Jaspers' argument that the psychopath cannot be properly diagnosed without a phenomenological analysis, I would add that one must also consider the culture within which the behavior and diagnosis occur. At the same time it is possible to believe that a more definitive system based on, e.g., cortical states, awaits the future diagnostician, although it seems to the writer that nothing better than a ratio of probabilities can be expected, since the sources of input to the diagnosis are so varied. Also, while we can agree with Hare that the various dimensions making up the syndrome may not yield to an interval scale interpretation, ordinal judgments, whether the measure is severity or number of relevant behaviors, do not seem a difficult projection. Clinicians use such a "weighted sign" system regularly in diagnosing (see Hammond, Hursch, & Todd, 1964).

Theoreticians of abnormality can proceed with their study of the psychopath without answering the question as to its fundamental nature, as is done with other syndromes such as cancer or schizophrenia. It is well to keep in mind however that excessive allegiance to one position brings the possibility of overlooking input to behavior variance from sources not congenial to that perspective.

Thus, type theory has tended to treat society as a given and as making little or no contribution to psychopathic behavior. To underscore the value of a quantitative perspective regarding psychopathy, I should like to discuss a related concept that (*a*) appears to have deep roots in the American culture; (*b*) has definitional elements not unlike psychopathy;

and (c) is typically represented as a quantitative phenomenon studied among the citizenry at large.

MACHIAVELLIANISM AND PSYCHOPATHY: CONVERGING DIMENSIONS

A sociopolitical tract that has been read for centuries and has at least indirectly inspired and directly supported the ruling style of countless heads of state was only as recently as a decade ago turned into an instrument of social psychology for studying interaction among men. One might wonder if this tardy translation of Niccolo Machiavelli's (1469–1527) princely manipulator from prose to empirical test required the special genius of American social psychologist Richard Christie and associates, or if the study of manipulation was an idea "whose time had come."

It is perhaps not easy to look into the potential gray area of power and manipulation, as C. W. Mills often noted, and Nader has recently (1976) reaffirmed. This is further attested to by the weak interest psychologists have shown in such exploration: Most references in the literature go back uneasily to Bertrand Russell (1938) or Alfred Adler. It is likely unsettling for investigators to root around in this pornographic realm where pulling strings to make others dance may be so titillating to the actor; power is exciting, dangerous. There is potential social dynamite in studying the way the average citizen might display manipulative behavior when he is indirectly asked about it, then given a chance to make good his beliefs.

Whatever the ground for the late appreciation of the everyday manipulator, it was not until 1964 at an American Psychological Association symposium that Christie unveiled his short, concise scale to measure what he has since called Machiavellian in interpersonal relations. He gives appropriate credit to Machiavelli himself, noting that the "Mach Scale" of 20 short declarative statements is based on the English version of the master's writings. Indeed, his book with Geis, *Studies in Machiavellianism* (1970) is dedicated to Machiavelli. Christie formulated a hypothetical role model of the Machiavel in terms of the following four characteristics:

1. A relative lack of affect in interpersonal relationships—manipulating should be enhanced by viewing others as objects.
2. A lack of concern with conventional morality—regarding lying,

cheating, and deceit in general, manipulators should have a
utilitarian view of interaction with others.
3. A lack of gross psychopathology—the manipulator is hypothesized to take a rational view of others and is in contact with
objective reality.
4. Low ideological commitment—he is more interested in tactics to
an end rather than inflexible striving for an idealistic goal.

The 20 highly discriminating items which sifted down to Mach IV[1]
are represented by such statements as "The best way to handle people is
to tell them what they want to hear," and "Honesty is the best policy in
all cases." The Machiavel would agree with the first of these and
disagree with the second. The scoring key was constructed so that the
Machiavel should agree with 10 items and disagree with 10, thus controlling for agreement response set. The scale produced from the outset
a suitable range of scores among college students and a national survey
of adults.

If Geis and Christie had only their scaled translation of Machiavelli in
hand, and the fact that persons differ nicely in extent of agreement–
disagreement, one might be impressed, but convinced of nothing in
particular. However, what gives the scale[2] its claim to validity is (a) its
relation to relevant behavioral indices, and (b) cross-cultural support.

Personality Correlates of the Machiavel

Christie and Geis (1970) found that when induced to cheat in an
experiment, both high and low Mach scorers indulged. What separated them was the capacity to look the accuser in the eye afterward:
The Machiavel looked his accuser in the eye much longer, while deny-
ing cheating. There are difficulties involved in realistically testing
(manipulating!) the Machiavel and his manipulative tendencies because of his general suspiciousness, which could readily be expected to
extend to experimental psychologists and their notorious covert
strategies. One solution to obtaining a behavioral measure that Christie
and Geis employed was to allow the experimental subject to be the
"experimenter." They put high and low scale scorers (U.S. college
undergraduates)[3] in a situation where they were to administer a test to a

[1] Mach V is a more psychometrically sophisticated multiple-choice version of the same
test.
[2] There is a "Kiddie Mach Scale" similar in composition to the adult version, and several
foreign language editions.
[3] Christie and Geis do not state this, but judging from the instructions offered and
general comments, subjects in these early studies appear all to have been male.

stooge person. It was emphasized to the subjects that they had total power over the testee (stooge) and were to use this circumstance to distract the latter's test performance. In a comparison of 14 high with 13 low scorers, the high scorers were twice as manipulative—defined by number of such acts perpetrated—as were low scorers, and were far more artful and creative in composing behavior designed to disturb the testee. On self-report follow-up, high scorers also indicated that they enjoyed the experiment more than low scorers, and specifically its manipulative aspects.

In order to investigate just how effective high scorers might be in manipulating others in a group, Christie and Geis constructed several bargaining games wherein the Machiavel could "show his stuff" in comparison with a low-scoring counterpart. In "The Ten Dollar Game" seven triads each containing a high, low, and middle Mach scorer were seated around a table on which lay 10 $1 bills. The money was to be given over to any *two* subjects who could agree on how to divide the total 10 dollars.[4] Subjects who were relative strangers to one another made up the groups for this one-trial play. As predicted, the highest scorers were able to differentially make it to the final coalition in all seven pairings. Low scorers on the contrary succeeded only twice in reaching the final pairs. High Machs averaged $5.57 winnings, middle scorers $3.14, and low, only $1.28 (Geis & Christie, 1970)—an experimentally neat matching of scale expectancies.

In evaluations of others, the student Machiavel seems to take a less favorable view than his low-scoring counterpart. This was true even of subjects taken from an American "church college," where relative love for one's fellows could be expected. After working in pairs on a difficult judgment task, subjects rated their partners on 20 bipolar trait descriptors, for example, interesting–dull and intelligent–unintelligent. In 19 of 20 possible comparisons, high Machs had a less favorable view of their partners than lows did of theirs. In the twentieth—shrewd, manipulative versus guileless, open—high Mach scorers saw the partner as more open and guileless than the low scorers did, a presumed positive, therefore uncharacteristic, judgment by the former. But it can be reasoned that from the point-of-view of the true Machiavel, this was also a negative judgment—only the naive or foolish are open and guileless.

Durkin (Christie & Geis, 1970) has viewed the low Mach as virtually another breed of organism from the high scorer. He employed a "ball and spiral game" where it was important for the two players to coordinate their efforts for the task of keeping the ball on the spiral ramp.

---

[4] A truly Machiavellian design.

Coordination required was so subtle and "momentary" that verbal feedback was no help with the task. Team scores of low Mach groups were greatly affected by the interactions among the partners, their mutuality. While overall measures of playing skill did not distinguish the two groups, the individual skill of high Mach scorers, rather than pair coordination, accounted for their team's performance. Based on his research, Durkin labeled the low Mach as "divergent," or affected in his responding by dynamic interactions with the human partner (environment). The high scorer by contrast is less personally involved, more cognitively tuned to the on-going situation—he maintains his individual orientation. The game behavior of the low scorers emerges from the relation to the partner:

> Low Machs treat others as persons; highs treat them as objects. . . . Encounter prone, lows know others by moving into contact with them. They do not stand off, maintaining the integrity of their own cognitive frame, but open up to and get carried away by the influence of the other [Christie & Geis, 1970, pp. 281–282].

The question of empathy and its relation to psychopathy was taken up in Chapter 4. In Abramson's (1973) study mentioned there, he found significantly higher "Mach tactics" scores among the graduate students in counseling training compared to other advanced psychology graduate students, and for the combined groups he found a significant negative correlation between the Carkhuff measure of empathy and "Mach tactics." Abramson expressed worry about the sorts of individuals who may be attracted to the potentially highly manipulative environment over which the counselor presides. Okanes found that senior-level students in a "business policy" class ($N = 97$) who scored high on Mach V ranked Rokeach Scale of Values adjectives "forgiving" and "honest" significantly lower and "imaginative" significantly higher than their low-scoring counterparts (Christie & Geis, 1970).

A picture begins to emerge from these studies in which the high Mach scorer can be seen as emotionally detached, behaviorally manipulative, skeptical of others, and cognitive rather than empathetic in orientation regarding a given situation and its mastery. It is not that high scorers are invariably more accurate than lows in judgments made in an interpersonal context. Rather they are less distracted by the presence of others, as Durkin demonstrated. In private, lows have shown similar ability to process cognitions (Christie & Geis, 1970, p. 304).

Recent research regarding the so-called "locus of control" and Machiavellianism has broadened the portrait drawn above. Christie and Geis (1970) had reported a correlation of .41 between external locus of control and Mach IV scores. Solar and Bruehl (1971) corroborated this, having found correlations ranging from .33 to .44 between Rotter's Internal–External (I–E) Scale and Mach IV for several groups of students in psychology classes. They account for this positive correlation by arguing that high Machs manipulate others from a feeling of powerlessness, an external orientation. Levenson and Mahler (1975), with a mixed-sex sample of 75 undergraduates, found that the more subjects felt controlled by powerful others the more they viewed others as untrustworthy ($r = .36, p < .05$) and nonaltruistic ($r = .29, p < .05$); the latter two measures coming from a Philosophies of Human Nature Scale devised by Wrightsman (Christie & Geis, 1970). Wrightsman had earlier found negative correlations of $-.67$ between Mach IV and trustworthiness, and $-.54$ for Mach IV and altruism (Christie & Geis, 1970, p. 42). Procuik and Breen (1976) offer added support regarding a relationship between a sense of being controlled by others and machiavellianism. They found a significantly higher correlation between Mach V and Levinson's "Powerful Others" measure (.41) than between Mach V and "chance control" (.09). This finding held only for male (University of Manitoba volunteers) students (female student correlations were all insignificant). Such studies need to be repeated with a wider sampling of cases in order to permit better delimiting of the major contributor to correlations found with the I–E Scale. It is noteworthy that the findings for women students are quite different from male student results, in those studies where sex was specifically mentioned. As Tajfel and Moscovici (1976) have recently pointed out, we have a theory of internal and external control regarding the individual, but little or none regarding the attitude baselines common to specific social groups.

SUMMARY OF PERSONALITY CORRELATES

Manipulation is a part of the definition of the Machiavel, but at the same time the high Mach scorers' tendencies in this direction as seen in cleverly constructed behavioral measures give construct validity to the attitude dimension. The Machiavel undervalues others in comparison with his low-scoring counterpart, and this is intensified the more he subscribes to a world view where others than himself seem in control. He does not judge others as trustworthy nor as concerned for others in an altruistic way: in an uncertain world where "others" make the decisions, a man is better off in viewing people as potential antagonists. High Machs evince suspiciousness of people, but less so of events or objects such as dice (Christie & Geis, 1970, p. 300).

The high Mach does not enter into relationships that produce mutual solutions to problems, or that proceed from dynamic interactions; he is psychologically "stand-offish" and oriented toward individual efforts and solutions.[5] In those imperfect measures of empathy which have thus far been obtained, the Machiavel scores poorly. He is not only relatively unmoved by others, he appears equally unaffected by his own beliefs and even his own behavior. Christie and Geis term this the "cool syndrome," wherein high scorers are rated less anxious by judges, show differential ability to successfully argue positions different from their own, and as noted, can lie while looking an accuser in the eye. Low Machs are by contrast a "soft touch."

This brief portrait shares distinct commonalities with the picture of the psychopath typically constructed by theorists. Indeed there seems hardly a single serious contradiction between the two profiles emerging from theory and research. "Manipulative," "distrustful," "self-oriented," "convincing," and "successful in interpersonal relations" are adjectives that describe both the psychopath and the Machiavel. At least a partial exception involves the rational stance of the Machiavel over against the psychopath. That is, whereas the psychopath appears in many ways to be rational, he often—perhaps in the more extreme cases—trips himself up. Manipulative, perhaps he is less cool about manipulating.

Christie and Geis (1970) report no relation between measures of psychosis or neurosis and Mach scores, and one would not anticipate such a relationship. The psychopath is in important ways the antithesis of the neurotic or psychotic, e.g., in contact with reality, and to the extent that the Machiavel shares behavioral variance with the former, neurosis and psychosis would be ruled out.

On the other hand comparisons with psychopathy seem until now seldom to have been made. One study with Peace Corps volunteers reported by Christie and Geis (1970) found no significant correlation between any of the MMPI scales and Mach. However these volunteers had been psychiatrically screened and scrutinized for pathology, which would effectively attenuate any correlations that otherwise might have been found. Smith and Griffith (1978) found that the MMPI Psychopathic Deviate scale did share significant variance with Mach IV scores. With a sample of 66 American college students (male and female, $\bar{X}$ age = 25.7 yrs.), Pd and Mach IV correlated .25 ($p < .05$).

---

[5]This is not contradicted in success in situations such as the "Ten Dollar Game." Although the high scorers succeeded here in pairing up successfully against low and middle scorers, this success again stemmed from an individualistic, impersonal standpoint, i.e., "I want to win something for myself and not be left out."

Society and the Machiavel

Christie and Geis express concern about the threat of broadening Machiavellianism:

> If our speculations are correct, modern society is becoming increasingly more similar in structure to the kinds of laboratory situations in which high Machiavellians win. Available evidence also suggests that individual orientations toward manipulation are increasing [1970, p. 358].

The following condensed research findings reported by Christie and Geis (1970) give substance to their concern and support a picture of increasing cynicism in the American population.

1. Mach scores in general increase from fifth and sixth grades up through the high school grades.
2. Preparatory schoolers produce higher Mach scores than do representative college samples.
3. Correlations between Mach IV and the Kiddle Mach scale ranged from .37 in the two dullest classes to .55 for the two brightest classes of sixth grade New York public schoolers.
4. High Mach 10-year-old Connecticut public schoolers were more behaviorally manipulative than were low scorers.

They conclude their work pessimistically:

> In summary, these college respondents were more Machiavellian in scale scores than adults in a representative national sample who had some college education as well as those who had none. In addition, within the adult sample, there was a negative relationship (significant beyond the .01 level by ANOVA) between age and Mach scores (Christie & Geis, 1968). . . . It is worth noting that of the three college samples collected in the fall of 1955, two had lower scores on Mach IV than *any* of the 14 collected nine years later in the fall of 1964 [1970, p. 377; italics in original].

If Machiavellianism is on the increase—and note that the business of Watergate and its effects on American attitudes *postdates* the concern of Christie and other investigators—the Christie and Geis compilation of research cannot make us optimistic about the picture in "free-wheeling America":[6]

> In general the more tightly we restricted the laboratory situation, as in modified Prisoner's Dilemma games in which the subject was playing a nonexistent opponent, had little latitude for improvisation, and there was little opportunity for irrelevant

[6]Weinrach and Ivey have recently discussed "the massive credibility gap" in U.S. society and they note Kelman's (1975) discussion of how subjects in experiments with psychologists learn "never to trust anyone" (1975, p. 264).

affect, the less well the high Machs did in relation to the low Machs. The more similar to the nonlaboratory world the experimental situation was, e.g., face-to-face contact, greater latitude for improvising behaviors, the more affectively complex the situation, the greater was the relative advantage of the high Machs [1970, pp. 342–343]. . . . Our general line of argument has been that the use of Machiavellian tactics enhances the exercise of legitimate power only if the rules of society are not so highly structured that there is little opportunity for innovative behavior [p. 343].

This is a powerful statement in support of the present author's argument for the importance of the broad social climate in which behavior displays occur: The looser the system, the more manipulative practices come into play. This would hold as well for "anomic environments," where there is less need to answer to anyone, e.g., to rural neighbors.

It may be that urbanization—with its typical result of throwing together many persons unknown to one another in fleeting, usually commercial contact—breeds conditions which enhance the potential for machiavellian behaviors. Guterman (1970) found among an Eastern United States sample of white-collar hotel employees that population of city and Mach scores were positively correlated.[7] Milburn found the same for young American female subjects ($r = 29$, Christie & Geis, 1970). A few cross-cultural findings support those coming from America. deMiguel's study of Spanish students age 16–18 found a correlation of .89 between Mach scores and a measure of industrialization in nine Spanish provinces where pre-university students were attending school and for the most part had always lived. Oksenberg found that Chinese students in a transitional situation, that of attending a Western school, obtained significantly higher Mach scores than those attending a traditional Chinese school in Hong Kong (Christie & Geis, 1970). In a Prisoner's Dilemma game Bethlehem found traditional Tongans made significantly more cooperative choices than those Tongans who "had Western experience" (determined by education, occupation, or domicile). Both male and female rural subjects chose more cooperatively than urban subjects (Bethlehem, 1975). Christie and Geis (1970) also reported a study showing a correlation of .40 between adjustment to the United States culture and Mach scores for Hungarian refugees. The use of control groups established that the relation was not a function of time spent in the United States, but apparently involved attitudes brought into the country. Are refugees who seek out America for asylum perhaps psychologically pretuned to U. S. cultural motifs?

An ironic twist to the work of Christie and Geis is the grudging admiration the Machiavel was able to elicit from these two liberal social

[7]This relation did not hold, however, for those subjects whose families instituted strong superego training.

science researchers. They confessed that their initial impression of the high scorer was very negative:

> However, after watching subjects in laboratory experiments, we found ourselves having a perverse admiration for the high Machs' ability to outdo others in experimental situations. Their greater willingness to admit socially undesirable traits compared to low Machs hinted at a possibly greater insight into and honesty about themselves [1970, p. 339].

They caution that their admiration is not unqualified. Their general attitude here shows close resemblance to the clinician's frequent grudging appreciation of the manipulating skills of the psychopath.

Two of the most fascinating findings thus far seen in the research into Machiavellianism involve the high scores obtained by persons in positions of considerable influence, and the view that slowly evolved out of Christie's theory of manipulativeness, namely that the Machiavel has a strangely rational view of his world and those who people it. The first of these judgments, should it prove as broad-based as Christie suspects, has the clear potential of actualizing an increasingly Machiavellian Western World through the value system of those who serve as keepers of the keys. Christie wrote

> In the years intervening between my first and second reading of Machiavelli, I had had a good deal of first-hand experience with people who were professionally involved in the control of others. Their roles varied from university presidents, deans, and departmental chairman to officials in the military and civil branches of government, to foundation executives, but there were noticeable similarities in their behavior. Given these experiences, a rereading of Machiavelli struck quite different chords. In terms of ability to dispense favors and privileges, these administrators were more closely akin to the Medici than anyone I had known prior to my first reading of Machiavelli [1970, p. 8].

The second point, obviously related, suggests that it is the manipulator who is in tune, and not those who officially deplore him. Like it or not, all world governments seem to be moving inexorably in the direction of top-heavy bureaucracies. Christie and Geis feel that a low Mach scorer would make prima facie a poor administrator because of his tendency toward personal involvement; and this just at the time that administrative positions are multiplying like hydra. It is tempting to suspect that the grudging admiration Christie and his coworkers have come to feel for the Machiavel is related to his potential when he is in a society that matches his lively tendencies; one which these researchers themselves share.

7

The Philosophy of
the Marketplace
and Psychopathy

A central thesis of this book has been that the social philosophy basic
to a given culture inevitably colors the process of diagnosing psychological problems. Although distressingly neglected by psychologists
when considering their own culture, variations in the collective psyche
of even the industrialized lands taken as a group are as stubbornly
obvious as they are stubbornly ignored. This bias is especially difficult
to justify for American psychologists, in view of the theory of man and
society dominant in North America. The empirical epistemology sub-
scribed to takes the empty organism for granted, thus assuring the view
that cultural factors have full play in human development. Little is made
of heritage and inheritance and the emphasis is on being active in the
present and making one's own future. The resultant egalitarianism is
heavily commited to the sanctity of the individual. But in spite of the
philosophical commitment to empiricism, which must anticipate vast
differences among persons maturing in lands where, e.g., caste systems
are formalized, or where commitment to the group is deemed more
important than to the individual, studies of national character differences by North American psychologists are declining decade by decade
(Nelson & Kannenberg, 1976). Even while intrepid American an-
thropologists such as Benedict, Mead, and Sapir have been leaders in

erecting a science of cultures emphasizing differences between rather than samenesses among peoples, American psychologists appear blind to their own cultural idiosyncracies and carry on blithely as if findings from researches based on American college students could casually be applied to humankind.[1] The desire to insure equality of opportunity seems in practice to have been translated to the sameness of persons, regardless of the sociopolitical system in which their behavior is embedded.

In the next several pages I want to detail some of the idiosyncracies of the American culture that seem to me to truncate seriously the building of a general theory of personality, and therefore of personality deviations, based on a U.S. model alone. At the same time I see cultural forces at work there which encourage behaviors typically labeled psychopathic, and these make the judging of the psychopath as ill or even antisocial a highly questionable practice.

EXPLORING NATIONAL CHARACTER

> Strictly speaking, the first empirical problem is to determine what modes of personality, if any, are present in a given society. Before this can be done adequately, however, we must define at least in a general way the conception of national character that is to guide our investigative efforts. Thus we have suggested that "national character" refers to *relatively enduring personality characteristics and patterns that are modal among the adult members of the society* [Inkeles & Levinson, 1969, p. 428; italics in original].

Inkeles and Levinson demonstrate with this quotation that they are prominent exceptions to those American theorists criticized above for unconscious ethnocentrism.[2] In discussing the process of studying modal personality, they have recommended examining (a) child-rearing systems; (b) collective adult phenomena; and (c) individual personality. I shall loosely follow this schema, taking a brief look into each area to illumine the pressures judged here significant to the development of the contemporary American character.

[1]There are often cautions noted by American researchers about generalizing from students to the (American) population at large, but no notice that one should not, for example, generalize to non-American students.

[2]Albee, in the article already quoted (1977), provides a cogent analysis and criticism of the changes in the American ethic from producing to consuming, but fails to mention any other potential economic strategies, e.g., Marxism.

Childhood Experiences

My intent here is to focus on relatively unique aspects of the contribution of American childhood to American character. At the same time I shall briefly consider informal observations and research data collected in other cultures.

IMPARTING VALUES

> Advertising has become all pervasive. It is as destructive of the Protestant ethic as all else added together. By the time a child is six, she or he has watched as many hours of television as a college student in classes earning a college degree. If the old saw is correct—that a child's mind is molded by age six—the hours and hours of commercials watched probably have more psychological impact than the college education [Albee, 1977, p. 158].

A recent U. S. critic found Saturday morning "children's hour" television:

> By actual count, 32 of the 59 commercials I saw in a four-hour period were for junk food. . . . Among the 18 ads for toys and dolls was one for "Nerf" footballs, those sponge-rubber superlight balls appropriate, one supposes, for kids too weakened from junk food to heft a real football. . . . For the girls, there are dolls who eat, drink, speak, wet, sneeze, and do everything except earn a college scholarship. . . . All in all, Saturday-morning television offers lots of nonsense, a little violence, and a continuous message to eat, eat, eat. . . . The Saturday-morning kiddie show is a dangerous baby sitter [Corcoran, 1975, p. 10].

Ward and Wackman (1973) found that about one-third of lower cognitive-level U. S. children (defined as those relying mainly on perceptual not conceptual cues)[3] think television commercials "tell the truth all the time [p. 129]." Liebert and Schwartzberg (1977) discussed a series of studies by Gerbner and Gross, indicating that both adolescent and adult American viewers who were heavy television users showed more belief in cultural and social stereotypes presented than did light users.

In the two Germanys, product peddling is confined to short announcements sandwiched around (never within) news reports and short entertainment pieces between 6:00 and 8:00 P.M. Few such messages are aimed specifically at the child as consumer, even in West Germany. England has only recently permitted a few private commercial television licenses, which by no means dominate the viewing

[3]The sample was 67 Boston children, 5–12 years old.

landscape. In both West Germany and England there are a wide range of cultural and entertainment programs, which do not avoid controversial themes, even during the afternoon children's programming. Spanish television has avoided within-show commercial messages.

Those Americans born early enough in the century to have missed this commercial television experience were subjected to a similar assault via radio when that instrument dominated mass communication. Lest a casual reader think the American child is somehow able to escape the consumer training of the media, it is not comforting to hear that the average U.S. television set runs 6 hours 15 minutes per day, which is about double the estimate for West Germany. Too, there is a greater percentage of homes outfitted with TV in America than anywhere else, and programming time is much more extensive than in Europe; for example East and West German programming ends typically at midnight, taking up again at 9–10 A.M., and commonly makes a complete afternoon pause between 1 and 4 P.M.

It is fashionable for critics of U.S. television to deplore the violence and vacuity of program offerings and their potential effect on the viewing audience (see nearly any edition of *The National Observer*). However I have found almost no mention of another possible system or cultural approach to this medium. It is as if one had no choice in America but to program as a popularity contest, where only those shows that are heavily viewed survive. The severest internal critics (cf. Winn in Shah, 1976) do not reach out for the experiences of other cultures with other methods of selecting programs. Research of differential effects of the very different television experiences of a German, French, or Spanish child seem seldom to be popularly discussed, let alone investigated; the basic values controlling the medium are left unchallenged. External critics, on the other hand, remark the social nature of the communication process—how it is affected by the society in which it occurs. Bisky (1976), of East Germany, argued that the profit motive contributes to the vacuous nature of American television, and serves to divert the working class viewer rather than to set him thinking, or to serve his, e.g., economic interests.

Cole (1976) made a comparative analysis of children's stories taught to mainland Chinese and the "Little Golden Books" which his own American students had been "brought up on." A thematic analysis yielded the following contrasts.

China	*U.S.*
1. Helpfulness and cooperation in pursuit of group goals	1. Individual goal seeking and achievement

2. Minimizing of roles defined by sex, age, or social prestige

2. Sex, age, and status roles often marked

3. Early introduction of the child into the adult world

3. Childhood often portrayed as a carefree period

4. Error seen as ignorance rather than stupidity or personality flaw

4. Naughtiness taken for granted and carelessness portrayed and punished

5. Care of personal and group possessions

5. Little attention given to care of material objects

Cole noted that his social psychology students easily see parallels between their own values and the themes of the American stories, as well as the contrast with the Chinese stories. Carrying the analysis to Henry Murray's well known list of needs, Cole felt that, for example, the need for achievement would require substantial re-definition when viewed in the light of Chinese values. "Gone is the emphasis on individual achievement. Instead, one extends oneself to achieve the goals established by the group [p. 3]. . . . Some needs never find any direct expression as felt needs in the Chinese stories because their fulfillment is as automatic as breathing. Need affiliation and need dependence are two [p. 4]." Concerning the presupposition that "moral stages" are "inexorable unfoldings" in the organism, Cole indicated that Kohlberg's higher stages might not even be viewed by the Chinese as representing desirable qualities.

Leichman (1975) repeated a study first carried out with children in Los Angeles ($N = 292$) by Weiner and Peter (1973). School children were presented with a hypothetical situation in which a child in a classroom is asked by the teacher to complete a jigsaw puzzle before the bell rings. There were three pieces of information regarding the hypothetical child: (*a*) He or she was either good or not good at working puzzles; (*b*) he or she either tried or did not try; and (*c*) he or she was either successful or not successful.

Leichman obtained a sample of 150 (75 male, 75 female) children, age 4–18 (paralleling the American sample), from the middle class of northern London. The test children were to award colored stars of varying values in judging the puzzle-solving behavior.

The California study had shown that American children below age 9 evaluated the *success or failure* of the pupil as the most important factor in assigning reward. By age 10, however, the *effort* of the pupil—his "trying"—took over as the main determinant of reward. Then at age 13 and continuing through age 18 (the top in the study) the outcome of

effort—again success or failure—reemerged as most important in judging the situation. Weiner and Peter contended that society reinforces
this more "primitive" developmental stage (1973, p. 290).

In the London group there were similarities to the American results
found, but also important differences. Ability of the "puzzle-solver," as
in the California study, played a minor role in gaining rewards from the
children. As in California, success or failure is the more rewarded
dimension for the children aged 4–9, and again at age 10 positive effort
emerged as most important. The major difference was that with the
English sample—and there were no significant sex differences—*effort
remained* the major factor in reward up through age 18, with no subsequent reversal to success–failure. There is as Leichman put it, no
"regression" to rewarding outcome as occurred in California. He titled
his study "Is it whether you win or lose, or is it how you play the
game?" and got two distinct answers from the two cultures. Leichman
speculated that Americans may be under greater cultural pressure than
the English "to come up with objective visible achievements [1975, p.
11]." One such pressure he mentioned is that concerning visible symbols of status. In the United States, where class is traditionally less
rigidly defined than in Britain, status is more clearly tied to measures
such as autos and swimming pools. The loosening of class lines in
Britain led Leichman to speculate that in the near future Britains too
may be more impressed with winning and losing than with how the
game is played.

Collective Adult Phenomena

The focus of this area of concern is the folklore of the culture:
magazines, films, and the morality they teach, as well as the measures
by which success and failure are gauged. In the America of a century
ago the hero was traditionally an uncompromising Frank Merriwell or
Horatio Alger hero who triumphed over adversity through persever-
ance and uncompromising honesty. According to Fortin:

> The major success writer in America's postbellum period was Horatio Alger. From
> the time of his first publication in 1869 of *Ragged Dick; or Street Life in New York with
> the Bootblacks* to his death in 1899, he was the most popular author in America. The
> Alger hero gave young people the formula for success. In an age of growing indus-
> trialization and material prosperity, the ragged boy could, by becoming more indus-
> trious, self-reliant, and frugal, prudently take advantage of the many opportunities
> afforded him and climb to the top of the economic ladder. In every Alger novel money
> was central to the plot [1976, p. B4].

Again the close of World War II seems to have heralded the demise of this selfless and persistent hero. The more modern hero accommodates the system; even when turning down a big-money job, as in the case of the hero of *The Man in the Gray Flannel Suit*. Our man did not suffer because of this seemingly unselfish decision however. He still got a "good" job from the boss and managed to sell inherited land for a lucrative housing development (Whyte, 1956). Contemporary lore shows the businessman as the slick interpersonal operator who satisfies his materialism in a veiled compromising way rather than through direct confrontation with economic forces.

William Whyte labeled this a change from the older Protestant Ethic to the new Social Ethic of organization life. As example of "a landmark in the shift in American values [1956, p. 243]," Whyte took the best-selling novel *The Caine Mutiny*, which he felt set the older value neatly against the new—individual responsibility versus "getting along in the system." The protagonist in this familiar tale is placed in the unenviable position of either relieving his incompetent superior officer who is a ship's captain, or doing nothing but follow orders, with the seeming certainty that the entire crew will be lost in a sea storm. The hero opts for responsibility by quietly relieving the captain. At a subsequent court-martial the hero is acquitted and the captain ruined. Later at a party the very defense lawyer who had brilliantly defended the hero reverses himself and says that hero and crew, not the captain, were in error, i.e., they should have served even an incompetent, covering his errors if need be, in the interest of "keeping the company going."

Noting that literary critics generally found the ending of this tale satisfactory, Whyte conducted an informal study to see how widespread this seeming substitution of compromise with authority for personal responsibility had become. He had 16 prep school boys write an essay on the central moral issue of the book. They were to decide how the author viewed the solution he had wrought and how realistic this solution was. By and large the boys grasped the basic moral issue of independence[4] versus the system, noted Whyte. The results showed that 15 favored the system, seemingly at any cost. Indeed some who had disagreed with author Wouk's perhaps uneasy solution (the men were,

[4]This study, indicating a trend away from individual responsibility toward serving the organization, may seem at first a move toward "group feeling" and a contradictory example to my thesis. However, on closer examination, independence here is a very responsible kind and involves the lives of one's fellows; it is not a sheer egoistic display in the sense of self-protection or self-expansion. Indeed the hero set himself up as a potential sacrifice for the good of all—in this sense extraordinarily "communal."

after all, acquitted) were inclined to be even harder on the mutineers than Wouk himself. Two typical comments make the point: "I cannot agree with the author in that I believe that one should obey orders no matter what the circumstances [1956, p. 247]." "Men have always been subjected to the whims of those in command; and so it will be in the future. This plan must exist or anarchy will be the result [p. 248]."

In light of the defenses made by ex-President Nixon's subordinates, which largely consisted of doing anything to get and keep the boss in power, the values of Whyte's prep schoolers back in the early 1950s become even more interesting. Well-placed Watergate defendants were in prep school at just about that time.

Individual Personality

American clinical–social psychology is replete with studies that characterize the American personality, although such revelations have usually been inadvertent by-products of studies having other purposes. As previously noted, such clinical–social studies are frequently reported as if humankind were the appropriate generalization group for results found. This has not been a deliberate act on the part of theorists and researchers, but inasmuch as the overwhelming bulk of research pours out of U.S. social science, and the longing is to create transhistorical theories, the caution of limiting results to the U.S. is simply buried. The recent discussion of a "crisis in social psychology" (an American crisis casually projected world-wide) is implicit recognition of the fleeting quality of research and theoretical paradigms often held as self-evident (see Gergen, 1973; Buss, 1975). In spite of (or perhaps because of) this ethnocentrism, coupled with a certain geographic isolation and the dominance of one language, certain personality correlates emerge as uniquely characteristic of the American culture.

That industrial societies in general require a certain punctiliousness and order in their citizens is an older notion of Fromm's. Failure to measure up to rigid requirements such as a regulated work schedule and regular attendance then produce guilt feelings or a sense of inadequacy in the properly socialized offender. As America has become more a consuming society than a producing one—parallel in time and motif with Whyte's (1956) concept of change from the Protestant Ethic to the Social Ethic—the themes important to personality formation have also changed. With the increase in advertising to encourage consumption of surplus, the concept of marketability has become current. Instead of merely anouncing via billboard or radio that a product was there to be purchased, the strategy became one of seducing the consumer to take what he really did not require, or to elect brand A over B whether or not there was any demonstrable difference between them.[5] This education in consumership[6] is more a product of media teaching than of the family, as our look at Saturday children's television programming demonstrated. Indeed the media have all but eclipsed the American family as teacher here, frequently standing at odds with parents, as occasional parent–advertiser confrontations have shown (Shah, 1976). It is in reality a short step from selling soap or cigarettes to selling personalities. Fromm spotted this change from about the time of its inception (cf. *The Sane Society*, 1955) and introduced the designation "marketing personality" in discussing it.

THE MARKETING PERSONALITY

Fromm has long scored the American obsession with selling and buying, carried so far as the buying and selling of one's most private possession, the personality. The self has come to be viewed as a commodity to be bartered in the marketplace, in Fromm's view. One tries on a series of roles for fit as one might various pairs of trousers. The personality to be sold must be in tune with the market and to the brand of personality in current demand. And in Fromm's view, as in my own, this interpersonal strategy is inculcated in the individual from kindergarten to college. Clausen (1957), in discussing delinquency and drug use, has employed the idea that the criminality and the psychopathic acting out seen among slum dwellers may in fact be a function of the inability of the ghetto dweller to "market" himself at a glorified level, leading to drugs and despair. Such a condition is not unlike that described by Durkheim (1961) for bachelors and divorced males in the context of suicidal potential. Because these men are not under the constraints of sex role demands common in Western monogamies, they "aspire to everything and are satisfied with nothing"—a condition also likely to produce anomie. Clausen's slum dwellers, along with the rest of the culture, are encouraged to seek riches for the purpose of becoming successful so as to enjoy unbridled consumption, and therefore also to aspire to everything and be satisfied with nothing. Through exploitation of wants via advertising, consumers are excited to a high pitch regarding ". . . what every man can and should accomplish in America. . . ." The unpleasant reality of the slum dweller's restricting

---

[5]Early ads for so commercial a product as Coca Cola merely showed a cold bottle of the liquid with the text: "the pause that refreshes."

[6]Perkins (1977) recently commented that the advertising printed all over U. S. clothing is the ultimate mark of the consumer age: The consumer has voluntarily become a walking billboard for the advertiser.

social possibilities may be an unbearable psychic burden, to be stunned and made less painful through drug use. In discussing the problems of American youth, Wolman has recently made a similar judgment: "Unfortunately in our society, even people of limited means have been influenced by the mentality of the upper classes [1975, p. 158]."

He laments the grotesque search for satisfaction of these upper-class "beautiful people" (p. 158), but unfortunately never inquires about what has led them to such compulsive hopping about after pleasure. Are they not also consumers who can aspire to everything and thus be satisfied with nothing? Why should they be immune to the cultural message which dominates the consciousness of those at other socioeconomic levels? Biskey mentions *"Waren fetischismus"* (1976, p. 171) in the West in criticizing social communications research, and suggests the theories elaborated have more to do with the persuasibility of American college students than with social influence per se.

It might be precisely the sense of inadequacy visited on anyone who fails to become rich or famous which accounts for that brand of psychopath which seems to emerge so consistently in the West and which we call the impersonator. This variety of psychopath (*Hochstapler*) is viewed by Kallwas (1969) as resulting from overidentification with an assumed role in which the subject can no longer distinguish the fantasy from reality.

Performances such as those of Kallwas' impersonator (*Hochstapler*) who must "appear more than he is" (*geltungsbeduerftigt*) raise the question of the basis for self-concept of persons so construed. Belaief sees self-esteem in the capitalist West as being largely a function of public performance, not only in one's work, but including as well sexual and intellectual power:

> In self-esteem of this sort we also noted the typical need and hope to be unequal and superior. Here equality implied failure to be superior to the average and held the threat of one's status being surpassed. This experience of self-esteem is never final and this produces continued anxiety and places others in the position of rivals rather than friends and lovers [1975, p. 32].

Inasmuch as we are all cajoled to try for the golden ring, why be surprised when someone like Frederick Demara takes the more radical approach of simply assuming the identity of someone who has "made it?" Marx is not so far off here if he sees capitalistic mechanisms as inherently alienating (cf. Kuvakin, 1976). As American philosopher Meyers has formulated:

> The Other encountered in a capitalistic world—whether it be a person, product, or nature—appears in an estranged form: it appears other than it really is. The Other I

confront in this society appears as an alien Other with which I have no essential bond, save the cash nexus. The Other in commercial society is a pimp for capital—a being (whether it be a commodity or a smiling merchant) disposed to seduce from me my economic essence—money. It is an environment of mutual suspicion, a society of calculating egoists, and in fact a civilized illustration of Hobbes' war of each against all [1976, p. 197].

A second form of self-esteem unlike the first is grounded on the value of existence apart from performance or achievement. Belaief refers the origins of this distinction to variational love from the mothering one in two broad kinds of societies. This second form of self-esteem is possible in a society where competition is less extolled; the first is not. "The tragic fact is that one is hoping to *earn* something which cannot be earned and must be given [1975, p. 34]." Where competition and superiority are extolled, according to Belaief, we are not able to care or wish for the well-being of another.

Social psychologist Morton Deutsch has recently argued that where economic activity is a primary social goal, it is inevitable that competition will dominate and that man will be seen as a commodity. He contrasts this with a "solidarity-oriented group," where values "emphasize personal ties to other members, group loyalty, mutual respect, personal equality, and cooperation [1976, p. 139]." Social scientists in Western societies have focused on equity, where rewards ought to be proportional to contributions, as one might expect under economic pressures. They have neglected equality, and have thereby, in Deutsch's view, contributed to the spread of economic values even to the noneconomic areas involving social relations, much as Fromm argued. Argyris too finds (1969, 1975) that the overwhelming values of decision makers in America, e.g., middle management corporate personnel, are to win, to inhibit interpersonal relationships and minimize interpersonal risk taking. Such persons were not refractory to change when challenged to be more open, truthful, and less reliant on norms of conformity and antagonism, although such behavior is rarely spontaneous among such groups in American society (Argyris, 1969).

Even the American scientist is not immune to the "marketing complex." A recent American Psychological Association *Monitor* newsletter carried an article on "The visible scientists." It is immediately interesting that Stanford University's communications department judged this topic worthy of doctoral study. The visible scientists like B. F. Skinner and Margaret Mead aggressively take advantage of the new communications media, we are told. The article states that during the 1950s and early 1960s visible scientists were "insiders" or men in science advocacy work in the government—plodders perhaps, but well placed.

Over the past decade, however, the visibility system has changed. The gadfly "out-sider" like Barry Commoner or Paul Ehrlich has emerged as the predominant archetype. These are "issue scientists," whose visibility is more ephemeral, depen-dent to some degree on fads [1975, p. 8].

THE ACHIEVING PERSONALITY

In America it is taken more or less for granted that achievement is a good, a valued thing. Indeed so powerful is the achievement ethic in America that any rejection of it is likely to be violent and excessive, such as occurred in the last decade when middle-class youth attempted to "drop out" entirely, in a kind of symbolic suicide replete with drugs, sexual excesses, and the creation of romantic utopias. A recent issue of the English newspaper, the *Daily Mail,* lamenting the cool attitude of the English toward "success," contrasted America:

But then, America esteems ability, actually makes something of it. Tiny Rowlands, boss of Lonrho, would have been hailed as another Carnegie, not the near-villain who inspired the phrase "the unacceptable face of capitalism." . . . Whether this is good or bad for artists is a moot point, whether they enjoy it or not depends upon the personality. But the point surely is this: in America people respond to success and achievement, celebrate it with unabashed enthusiasm and are eager for more [Gib-bins, 1977, p. 6].

Achievement of some philosophic plateau or intangible educational goal would not fulfill this ethic in the minds of most denisons of the culture. Education should itself bring something tangible, e.g., a degree guaranteeing increased earning power. "Improving one's mind," banal as it is when so formulated, rates in public approval well below the increased earning and social prestige that education is expected to bring.

In this context it is no accident that the achievement motive has been institutionalized through the work of American researchers McClelland and Atkinson. McClelland has progressed beyond mere measuring of the motive to the creation of a program to instill it in persons such as business managers, whose careers assumably would be abetted with increased achievement motivation. He has recently set about exporting it to other cultures (cf. McClelland & Winter, 1969). McClelland has tied the construct explicitly to economic growth:

What is the evidence that n Ach is a key factor in economic growth? . . . The n ACH content of popular literature has been shown to have increased on several occasions prior to rapid economic growth in a country and to have declined prior to a slacken-ing in the rate of growth. When n ACH content is coded among modern nations in children's textbooks, those countries that scored higher in n ACH in 1925 and again in 1950 subsequently developed at a faster rate economically than countries that scored lower [1969, p. 11].[7]

What type of man is the achiever? He is more than normally interested in concrete feedback, McClelland says, and thus is akin to businessmen who tend to get *concrete feedback* of *concrete performance* (my italics): ". . . the man with high n ACH thinks of money as a concrete symbol of how successful a man has been, rather than as a motivator [1969, p. 58]." Eminent scientists, by contrast, are not high scorers. McClelland also predicted that entrepreneurial business execu-- tives would universally score higher on n ACH than educationally comparable professionals, and so they do.

The strategy of measurement of n ACH is familiar and simple. McClelland and coworkers take a modified version of the TAT and score stories composed by the experimental subject for the presence or absence of themes judged by the researchers to indicate achievement motivation. Following success in the United States, McClelland introduced a training course, with the approval of the Indian government, to increase n ACH of Indian leaders from small industry and commerce in just 10 days. In training the men were taught to code their own stories written to the stimulus pictures. Later they rewrote the stories in an effort to improve their a ACH score. They were coached in this effort by the seminar staff. Case studies were scrutinized and model achievers charted for the student. Dependent measures of success were changes in business activity of the men and their economic performance measures. In a 2-year post-course follow-up, experimental subjects did show significantly greater entrepreneurial activity than control subjects. This increase took the form of such actions as production and firm expansion, increased income and capital investments, and a greater labor force in the entrepreneur's charge.

The underlying rationale of McClelland and his staff has been that men (I have not seen work with women reported) normally seek to maximize their own interests, and in a fairly direct fashion, an antici- pated hypothesis vis-à-vis the value system from whence the research- ers come. Although not necessarily focussed on wealth or prestige, these are anticipated byproducts for those high in n ACH. While one is impressed with the results obtained, especially in so short a time, it is our interest to examine the implications of an effort such as this in the context of the individual and his cultural values.

[7]Reprinted with permission of Macmillan Publishing Co. from *Motivating Economic Achievement* by D. C. McClelland © 1969 by The Free Press.

In addition to the assumption that it is natural to seek one's own maximum pay-off, it is also implicit that "economic advance" is prima facie a good thing. A psychologist–reviewer of the McClelland book *Motivating Economic Achievement,* for example, discussed the training in India very positively:

> It shows that the possibility of *improving a society* by producing changes in its people deserves careful and continuing exploration and that its payoff may be much greater than is obtained from the provision of hardware and money [Wallace, 1969, pp. 638, 640; emphasis added].

It can and has been as easily argued that there are severe limits to how far economic growth can be driven before a land—or planet—suffers. That spawning courses in the "salesman–entrepreneur" direction (McClelland & Winter, 1969, p. 58) might reflect short-term gain and long-term difficulty seems not to have occurred to the reviewer above. Witness the severe competition for markets among some entrepreneurial states, for example the United States and Japan, or the armament sales race currently under way. Rudin looked at need achievement from the more balanced point of view that it might produce undesirable psychological effects in a society as well as desirable. He took measures of psychomorbidity, that is, death rates seemingly due to aggressiveness (murder, suicide, and alcohol) and those due to "inhibition" (ulcers, hypertension). The United States was one of the highest on both counts.

> Using McClelland's 1925 data (motivational scores) on needs for achievement and power (latter to dominate, influence and direct others) of 16 societies, power and aggressiveness (1950 death rates) correlated Rho = .42 (p slightly greater than .05). The need for power is seen as correlated with the acting out of impulses and with a manipulative, aggressive attitude toward other people. I infer also a loss of humane values and a willingness to engage in violence (as exemplified in murder and suicide) [Rudin, 1971, p. 463].

Perhaps even more important is the related argument that man ought to strive to maximize the satisfactions of his communal group and be less concerned with his own personal gain, and that this will serve the long-term interest of humankind. This point has been broached repeatedly by research and theory in the present volume, and is at the base of many highly valued human ethical systems.

Block (1973) used Bakan's "two fundamental modalities . . . of all living form: agency and communion [p. 515]," as constructs within which to discuss masculine and feminine ideals among male and female college students of six countries, America, United Kingdom, Sweden, Denmark, Finland, and Norway. She first defined these constructs:

> Agency is concerned with the organism as an individual and manifests itself in self-protection, self-assertion, and self-expansion. Communion . . . is descriptive of the individual organism as it exists in some larger organism of which it is a part and manifests itself in the sense of being at one with the other organisms [1973, p. 515].

She used a concept of: "idealized-self—the description of the kind of person I would most like to be [p. 519]" as an indicant of the prevailing cultural definition of the ideal male and female. Four psychologists rated the self-descriptive adjectives used for their relation to the definitions of agency and communion. Block found distinct cultural differences:

> American males are distinguished, at or beyond the .05 level of significance, from the males of other countries by placing greater emphasis on the following adjectives: adventurous, self-confident, assertive, restless, ambitious, self-centered, shrewd, and competitive in their conceptualizations of the masculine ideal—adjectives reflecting greater agency. Interestingly, American women also described their ideal in more agentic terms than did women in the other countries studied. The descriptions of the American feminine ideal incorporated to a significantly greater extreme the following adjectives: practical, adventurous, assertive, ambitious, self-centered, shrewd, and self-confident. The greater endorsement of agentic adjectives by American students, both males and females, goes along with Bakan's suggestion of a relation between capitalism and agency [p. 520].

She further noted that Sweden and Denmark, which she characterized as well-established social welfare states, showed fewer sex differences and less emphasis on agency than the other lands studied.

HYPERBOLE AND CULTURAL EXCESS

P. T. Barnum may not have originated the American fondness for hyperbole, but he can stand as a representative figure in a stream of advertisers who have scrambled over one another in employing new superlatives for wares to be sold to the point where the superlative is in danger of having its meaning completely stripped away. Thus one can now be "thrilled," we are told, via ubiquitous billboard advertising, by supping on "brand X" sausage. While sausage is doubtless a pleasant-tasting dish, it is difficult to equate it with anything approaching the original meaning of "thrill," which implies at the very least a sharp sense of excitement. The most mundane of canned or prepackaged foods become heavenly, captivating, divine in the lexicon of the word huckster. The words for the truly rare exhilaration, the "peak experience," have been stolen, raped of their meaning, and left for dead—strewn among the ashes of consumer advertisements.

The already lavish hyperbole contained in the designation "star" will no longer serve as depiction for entertainers from professional sport or films, but has through careless use been so cheapened that "super star" had to be created to cover the former preserve served by "star." Now the journeyman actor or baseball player inherits the "star" mantle. With more and more superstars on the word magician's horizon, something like the designation "nova" or "super nova" would seem less than remote. In German there is no comparable concept. That is, an actor is simply an actor, better or less well-esteemed. Today the French and Germans also resort to the English "stars," having never employed this form of hyperbole in their own tongues.

This fetish for superlatives seems rooted in part in America's very picture of itself. If one hasn't something in his home city or town that isn't the world's widest, longest, hottest, coldest, or strongest, one's very identity is suspect, or one is a dreaded Number Two. The self-congratulatory excesses of the recent 200-year jubilee seem to have exhausted the patience of even the most sanguine observers. This record-keeping hyperbole falls remarkably easily from the tongues of politicians who are continually noting that, for example, in this term of office more of X, Y, or Z was produced, sold, consumed, etc., than ever before. While politicians the world over exaggerate the quality of their contributions to their people and the world, in listening for years to foreign-language media broadcasts, I have seldom heard "the world" invoked as a measure of the value or importance of one or another country's accomplishments. This is not to deny national pride over something like Olympic Game victories in Eastern lands. But events of this stature are indeed "world measures."

In any case—and admitting I have not listened to a random selection of foreign broadcasts—this misuse of the superlative is not confined to American politicians and press agents. Thumbing through even something as conventional as college "news for alumni," one readily comes across something like the following:

> Dr. _____, 38, will head _____, the fourth largest magazine in the country, which is owned by The Charter Company, a multi-industry company listed at 173 on this year's Fortune 500 Directory. Named one of the Ten Outstanding Young Men in America in 1971 by the U. S. Jaycees, Dr. _____ leaves his six-year post at the 11,000 student institution in Miami where, in 1969, at age 32, he created the school and became the youngest state university president in the nation. Opening with more than 5,000 students, Florida International had a higher first year enrollment than any other institution of higher learning in the United States [*At Bowling Green*, 1975, p. 5].

Dr. _____ may be and probably is all of these things, but the emphasis is clear: He is a series of records. On the very same page of this "alumni news" we are told that the editors of the *Guinness Book of World Records* confirmed that 3376 snake dancers at the university broke all previous records for a snake-dance chain. Or take this example from a highly regarded weekly newspaper:

> The HOTTEST [sic] politician in America today is 37-year-old Edmund G. "Jerry" Brown, Jr., the Democratic governor of California. When he became governor almost a year ago, most people expected he would be a liberal in the tradition of his father, Edmund G. "Pat" Brown, governor of California from 1958 to 1966. But Jerry Brown has been a surprise. He attacks government. He questions all kinds of assumptions and values. And, politically, it works. Almost 90 per cent of the people in California applaud his performance, an extravagant tribute. He's a bachelor, living in a bare apartment in the state capital. He rides around in a Plymouth, not a limousine. He says things no politician has ever said before, including some things no politician has ever thought about before. In an age of political conformity he is special. Already, people are talking about him as President some day [*The National Observer*, 1976, p. 12].

Examples of such rhetorical excess could be multiplied without a great deal of searching, and in themselves may seem unremarkable. What I am arguing is that this obsession with bigness and betterness has contributed, because of its very excess, to a decline of recognition of performances depicted as merely average or normal in the statistical sense, and to a craving for the exaggerated, the extreme. It is as if one must be at the adjectival extreme to be heard. The disingenuousness emerges when the inevitable average or below average performance is patched over with hyperbole. In this competitive society, if some are to reach the pinnacle, others must fail, or at any rate settle for a lesser level. Rather than accepting the average for what it is, such recognitions are taboo, and are wished away with Orwellian labeling tactics. Journalists seem to have the same need to seduce the reader with absurd claims that distinguished the case of John in Chapter 2. Mr. Brown is likely a promising governor, but it is doubtful that he has thoughts that have never been thought before.

When coupled with the press for material achievement already noted, the psychopath's bidding for attention at any cost, his casual treatment of the truth in pursuit of personal ends can hardly be regarded a shocking endproduct. One sells oneself and others just as any product, by arranging for unlimited and unstinting praise.

THE PSYCHOPATH AS RATIONAL

If we assume for the moment a culture that, even if covertly, applauds and basically reinforces behaviors that fit hand-in-glove with behaviors that under other circumstances earn the label "psychopath," then a judgment of insanity, or even maladjustment, cannot be easily made. My plea up to this point has been to make the case that the psychopathic-like may be the more truthful, or at least the more accurate, reader of the important values of the culture than those who profess to abhor him. I wish now to add to my own some judgments from those who have had varying experiences with the psychopath.

William Sheldon, usually only mentioned in connection with the constitutional argument regarding abnormalities, had in fact as early as 1949 shown a remarkable respect for the situation of the young delinquents whom he studied. Sheldon even went so far as to side with the "predatory delinquent" against society:

> They saw human society in a truer light and were more truly engaged with life than were most of their elders who were professedly engaged in dealing with "delinquency" but in fact were concerned mainly with their own security and righteousness [1949, p. 829].

These delinquents were not wrong in orientation, in Sheldon's view, merely inept at execution. Presumably given more maturity or social connections, they would have been celebrated rather than incarcerated. While discussing the more general concept of delinquency, Sheldon noted how students of delinquency have failed to take into account what he called the delinquency of institutions. As example he referred to an American army major of his acquaintance whose civilian company deliberately manufactured razor blades that would wear out quickly, and noted that this man would never be judged delinquent by American society for such behavior. While deceptive, it is after all "good business."

The finding that the psychopath is difficult to condition has led to the hypothesis that difficulty in learning social norms is constitutionally based (see Chapter 3), but in the absence of more definitive evidence, may be as easily explained on a social basis. That is, the alert child simply learns to parrot the values (Cleckley's "words without the music") that the naive take seriously and the cognoscente snicker at, and puts his trust and effort in the covert but real values which shake and move the culture. The McCords indirectly confirm this view: The psychopath sees nothing wrong with himself, therefore no reason to change (1964, p. 118). Cleckley's pessimism concerning treatment may turn on the same point. Hare has quoted Arieti's view that the "complex psychopath" operates on the basis of what "is or is not socially acceptable from a rational point of view instead of from an emotional one [Hare, 1970, p. 103]." Like the Machiavel, he does not let empathy get in his way. Preoccupation with self-interest also matches a psychopathic *modus operandi*. Certainly the psychopath, with his casual disregard of the humanity and basic rights of others, would have to be in favor of a "do your own thing" philosophy. His unbridled egoism makes him a model figure for a philosophy stressing "every man for himself." Szondi (1952) quotes existentialist Strauss as believing that the true sign of perversion in human relationships is the destruction of tenderness. This could seemingly as well apply to a society as to an individual. Once again the psychopath may only represent the extreme of a continuum along which general self-interest is prime, and other values take a secondary, or even antagonistic place.

Recently a few social scientists in the United States have been critical of this one-sided individualism, against which group goals and group feeling suffer such short shrift (cf. Bronfenbrenner, 1975; Campbell, 1975; Hogan, 1975). Hogan views dimly the cult of individualism, and its romantic (Rousseau to Rogers) egocentrism (Hobbes to Freud), which celebrates the individual fighting against, or at least perfecting himself against, society. While not gainsaying inherent competitive tendencies in the person, he argues that the need for helpful, trustful interaction with one's fellows is also basic. Bronfenbrenner, after extensive cross-cultural research into developmental norms, has also expressed concern over U. S. norms of interpersonal behavior:

> A few months earlier, I had just returned from a research trip to Eastern Europe, Israel, and Scandinavia, and was about to report to a group of my colleagues on what had impressed me most: the cooperation and concern for others I had observed among children, and, even more, the commitment, on the part of the adult society, to children and those responsible for their care. The commitment was manifested not only at the governmental level in terms of health, education, and welfare services, but also in the everyday behavior of people in all segments of the society; compared to us, they appeared to care more about those who could not care for themselves. As I was reviewing my thoughts on these matters, I heard the chairman conclude his introduction: "And now, here is Urie Bronfenbrenner," he said, "to do his own thing" [1975, p. 4].

Without concerning ourselves with the merits of emphasizing community versus individuality as such, I would only remark that in a situation where individualism is trump, the psychopath is powerfully equipped to survive, if not always to succeed. That is, if the operational basis of the culture requires projecting a good image while watching out for oneself, if it encourages pursuit of material pleasure and the merchandizing of people, then far from being a mask of sanity or a moral imbecile, the pychopath is the reasonable one and those of us who are trusting, reliable, and empathic are out of phase with reality.

As deFundia, Draguns, and Phillips (1971) argued in advancing their caricature theory (see Chapter 8) of culture's relation to general psychopathology, abnormal behavior is only seemingly outlandish and bizarre. In fact it represents culturally shared behavior modes, wrongly applied. With the psychopath the discrepancy is even less than with, say, schizophrenia. Nonpathologic, hence undiagnosed, varieties of abnormal behavior may be as important as those identified by psychiatric services, a point of Jablensky's (1976) with which I strongly concur.

Lange-Eichbaum, in a work concerning genius, madness, and fame (1942), discussed along with the commonly mentioned varieties of psychopath such as the aggressive and inadequate, a third—the creative. He has pointed out how sometimes the psychopathic temperament, while under other circumstances disrupting, can be highly integrated. For example his unrest and imaginativeness drive the psychopath to broad undertakings, to variegated experience, thus giving his talents full play (p. 279). Such a subtype is rarely discussed today (particularly in the English literature), perhaps because of the emphasis on psychopathy as defect.[8] Such a category would seem congenial to those cases mentioned here who achieve fame and success in the culture— that is, persons who are able to use the functional norms of the culture to their own best advantage and circumvent legal trouble in the bargain, even when officially frowned upon for employing "caricatured means.[9]

[8] A recent study by Nelson and Farley (1976) relates to this point. A hypothesis was advanced which seeks to relate delinquency and creativity through the mediation of the previously discussed (Chapter 3) arousal- and stimulation-seeking motives. Specifically it is argued that, given arousal deficit in Western teenagers, if the environment is rich in socially approved stimuli, creative behavior results; if impoverished, the arousal-deficient child will find socially disapproved outlets. With a sample of 205 Canadian eighth and ninth graders (male and female), there was a substantial trend in the direction that those who were low on an arousal measure and high in stimulation seeking differed on creativity and socialization (Gough's socialization scale) measures, depending on their socioeconomic status (SES). On all measures the higher SES group had a higher mean creativity score.

[9] Here I am reaching beyond Lange-Eichbaum, who was inclined to see the psychopathic process as distinct from the gift of genius—although present within the same person. I am suggesting that where culture and genius meet, e.g., in emphasizing capital accumulation, the processes are complementary.

8

Psychopathy in Varied Cultures

PROBLEMS OF CROSS-CULTURAL DIAGNOSIS

There may be numerous ways in which disorders will be influenced by cultural differences. One might find differences in the actual prevalence of cases between cultures. Or there may be no overall differences between cultures but only differences in the relative frequency of varying types of problems. Such frequencies could of course be further influenced by inconsistent diagnostic practices between cultures. Even more subtle, the actual impairment of function, hence one's probability of being brought to the attention of mental health authorities, depends in part on cultural expectations and the support of the sufferer provided by the given culture. Cultures too, for their own reasons, might be reticent about "owning up" to certain diagnostic categories. Thus it would be folly to discount sociopolitical factors in judging aspects of normality–abnormality across cultures. Finally a recent World Health Organization (WHO) seminar on the Personality Disorders (1972) noted the probable existence of culture-specific personality disorders.

To this point I have reassessed the traditional view of psychopathy as mere "failed socialization," and have arrived at what I believe to be the more realistic picture of a syndrome that is in many ways highly adapted to societies whose values share variance with it. The person who finally becomes judged a psychopath in such a society must step sharply over the boundary of "normality" in order to become visible, or alternatively hold a weak position vis-à-vis those providing the diagnosis.

It is sooner or later incumbent on my argument to examine aspects of the psychopathic personality as manifested in cultures ostensibly differing from one another in their philosophies of man. Let me emphasize the word "ostensibly" here, since just as America professes Christian values of charity and fellowship and in reality achieves something quite different, even opposite, so other cultures cannot necessarily be relied on to meet the obligations of their idealism. In comparing nations I must warn that limitations of source, language, and reporting systems place severe restrictions on data presented. For example, even within two relatively similar societies such as America and West Germany, one recent German theorist finds subtle yet not unimportant linguistic distinctions relevant to diagnosing. Thus Kallwas (1969) finds the shared descriptor "impulsive" (German: *impulsiv*), in common use among Anglo-Saxon labelers of the psychopath, to be "somewhat too aggressive" for the German understanding and hence not exactly suitable for direct translation. Saenger (1968) finds the German *einsam* to have more "heroic undertones" than has "loneliness," its English equivalent. Even where language differences are not at issue, idiosyncracies loom large. Cooper (1970), in a cross-cultural study of English and American diagnostic practices, found the American "category width" much broader than the English in arriving at a diagnosis of schizophrenia, which he felt accounted for the higher percentage of schizophrenics in American than in British institutions. When one considers cultures as diverse as America, Russia, and the Federal Republic of Germany (D.D.R.), and the potentially more political nature a diagnosis of psychopathy carries, compared with schizophrenia, for example, it is clear that the buyer must beware.

From a scientific standpoint, it would be ideal if investigators could go into different lands, start from commonly agreed-on definitions, administer appropriate controls, and relate responses obtained to important cultural themes. Obviously available information on potential psychopathic cases can make no pretense to such an ideal. One is indeed hard-pressed to locate even the most banal data for use in cross-cultural comparisons. A major block, for example, is that many sources simply do not break down incidence statistics to the level of the category "psychopathy" or "antisocial personality."[1] Instead the psychopath is buried amid the Personality Disorders (ICD-8, 301) many of which differ in very fundamental ways from psychopathy, as already suggested. Too, definitions of syndromes, even when on the rare occasion available, are far from equivalent. This problem was a major theme during the WHO Tokyo seminar (1972) concerned with diagnosis, classification, and statistics of the Personality Disorders in general. The strategy of this seminar was to have the conference participants rate 10 case histories of patients, some of which were chosen as typical Personality Disorders, others because they were doubtful cases. The diagnosers were given substantial background information on each case and asked to code it using ICD-8. They were asked to list alternative diagnoses and to indicate which information from the case history was most important to them in determining the diagnosis reached. Results of these international cases (although the bulk of the cases were Japanese) judged by an international panel of psychiatrists indicated some substantial differences in diagnostic labels affixed. There was serious hope expressed that improvements to ICD-9 might lead to more solid agreement. In spite of the magnitude of the problem of standardizing this diagnostic category, the participants were in general agreement on the importance of this goal for both national and international purposes (Shepherd & Sartorius, 1974; WHO, 1972).

Some Considerations of Definition

In the 1952 edition of the *Diagnostic and Statistical Manual of Mental Disorders* (DSM-I) of the American Psychiatric Association, the psychopath was listed as a Sociopathic Personality, Antisocial Reaction (000-x61). This specifically American diagnosis emphasized failure to profit from experience and punishment, failure of loyalty, with emotional immaturity, lack of judgment, and a facility for rationalizing behavior so that it would appear reasonable.

In an effort to come more in line with international nomenclature, the United States participated in the eighth ICD revision under the auspices of WHO in 1963. The international perspective now places the psychopath, as noted, under the Personality Disorders as an Antisocial Personality. The diagnostic description reads as follows:[2]

[1]In the International Classification of Diseases (ICD-8) the Antisocial Personality is numbered 301.7.

[2]Jablensky notes that ICD-9 has kept the same Personality Disorders because "a WHO seminar on the subject concluded that there is no sufficient new knowledge on which to

Includes a personality disorder characterized by disregard for social obligations, lack of feeling for others, and impetuous violence or callous unconcern. There is gross disparity between behavior and the prevailing social norms. Behaviour is not readily modifiable by experience, including punishment. People with this personality disorder are affectively cold and may be abnormally aggressive or irresponsible. The tolerance to frustration is low; they blame others or offer plausible rationalizations for the behaviour that brings them into conflict with society [WHO, 1974, p. 41].

It is evident that the emotional immaturity criterion from DSM-I has a highly subjective ring for grounding a diagnosis. In the writer's view its absence from DSM-II (1968) after the international collaboration matches more closely to the reality of the oft socially successful psychopath. In fact DSM-II specifically tries to avoid a "loser" image of the psychopath by ruling out the diagnosis because of "a mere history of repeated legal or social offenses [DSM-II, 1968, p. 43]." This could, at least in theory, permit a recognition of the "successful psychopath" more readily than the older definition, and squares more with European theorists (cf. Henderson, 1939; Kallwas, 1969; Lange-Eichbaum, 1942; Schneider, 1940).

While the earlier American system (DSM-I) distinguished a "dyssocial sociopath" as a criminal type capable of stong group loyalties, in the reality of handling cases this category seems to have played at best a minor role and the diagnosis has little international standing. As expressed by the Tokyo WHO conference, it would be highly desirable if international agreement on criteria for the Personality Disorders could be reached, among them of course our specimen the psychopath. Only then would a discussion of cross-cultural incidence rates begin to take on significant meaning. As things now stand such comparisons are extremely hazardous. In the Soviet Union Sukhareva has provided a listing of types of psychopathy (Rollins, 1972). One sees that they span traditional Personality Disorders, with some added diagnoses as well.

The psychopathic subtypes in Table 8.1 emphasize the physiological posture of the Soviet view of psychopathic states. The search there for the bases of abnormal behavior has typically been carried on at the level of brain pathology (Luria, 1957). Thus a tendency to impulsiveness and lack of inhibition is presumed grounded in early brain damage. A case observed by Rollins (1972) of a 14-year-old sexually preoccupied boy, given to masturbating in public, is indicative. He also had the dangerous habit of inhaling gasoline fumes. He was diagnosed a Personality

---

base a modification of this scheme [1976, p. 6]." At the same time he notes that a new category to ICD-9, 312, should be an advantage for coding aggressive, destructive behavior and delinquency not elsewhere classifiable.

TABLE 8.1
Varieties of Psychopathic Disorder[a]

Psychopathy (pathological development of the personality)
A. Infantilism: Inhibitions of development
    1. Instability
    2. Excitement
    3. Hysteroid
    4. Pseudologia
B. Disproportional (distorted) development—Genetically determined
    1. Cyclothymic personality
    2. Schizoid (autistic) personality
    3. Psychasthenic personality
    4. Paranoid personality
    5. Epileptical personality
C. Damaged development—Intrauterine or postnatal brain damage
    1. Failure of inhibitory controls
    2. Impulsive excitement

---

[a]Data are from G. E. Sukhareva, in Rollins, 1972.

Disorder and his problems attributed to "early organic insufficiency" on the evidence of EEG dysrhythmia. Interpersonal factors were largely dismissed. Rollins felt that there were obsessive–compulsive features in the case that were ignored. Freudian motives stemming from uncertain internal origins are officially (and largely, unofficially too, it seems) ignored by Soviet theorists.

Rollins tells us the influential psychiatrist Myasischev regards behaviors such as lack of positive interests, hostility toward school, authority, and the child collective, and impulsiveness and cruelty to be a result of educational failure (pedagogical error).

Regarding incidence rates of psychopathy it is by no means clear what hypothesis would derive from the expectations of cultural differences thus far discussed. Should, for example, a culture like that of the United States, which we have argued encourages psychopathy, have fewer psychopaths than, say Poland, because of greater tolerance for what may be a more modal behavior? Or more of them, since it could be argued that with more people "practicing" the behavior, more should also overstep than in less nourishing cultures? It is clear that there are too many unknowns, too many "ifs" to make meaningful cross-cultural comparisons at this time. What I shall do is present some relevant research data from various countries illustrating differences in behaviors believed to have relevance for the diagnosis of psychopathy, and later provide those published incidence figures which I have been able to obtain.

RESEARCH ON PSYCHOPATHIC BEHAVIORS

The Hutterites

While strictly speaking a culture within the American culture, the Hutterites have been able to so isolate themselves from modern Americana that they represent a unique cultural experiment. In fact, like the Amish sect, they undoubtedly share less with the American culture than do lands of Western Europe, where the modes of American popular culture have a pervasive contemporary influence. As Eaton and Weil (1955) describe them, the Hutterites are an isolated Anabaptist sect living principally in the American middle west. They live a simple, rural existence, in notable harmony, and provide all community members with economic security regardless of their circumstances. They originated among Germanic people who had lived together in neighboring villages in Europe for a long time before migrating to the United States from southern Russia between 1874 and 1877. Their life style emphasizes pacificism, simple living, and communal property; what they own is in the name of the church. The group takes precedence over the individual in what might be called a "religious socialism." They are in many ways a microcosm of certain values held basic to socialist theory.

What kinds of problems does such a society reflect? Eaton and Weil examined the case records of all 8542 community residents (living there in 1950) and summarized as follows:

> In projective psychological tests the Hutterites, like other groups, show antisocial and aggressive impulses, but in their daily lives they repress them effectively. Their history showed no case of murder, arson, severe physical assault or sex crime. No individual warranted the diagnosis of psychopath [1955, p. 235].

While not wishing to denigrate the Rorschach, which I believe to be a legitimate tool for researching personality, I think the significant findings are at the behavioral level, and I would suggest that this culture is doing something right vis-à-vis psychopathic and related antisocial behaviors.

Western versus Eastern Children

On Rollins' (1972) observations, conventional contemporary Western forms of acting out, while not unknown, are of little significance numerically in the Soviet Union. Thus drugs and "hippiedom" were minor considerations. Her impression, perhaps contrary to some Western presuppositions, is that there is more tolerance of deviant emotional states than in the United States (although not to the extent of condoning hostile acting out); in particular, she felt that "love states" are easier to accept there. Where interpersonal relations are concerned:

> Another aspect of communist morality emphasizes the obligation of the individual, within the collective, to help one's neighbor, so that the achievement level of the group as a whole would be raised. Thus, on the one hand, mutual assistance is encouraged. In school, the more gifted students are expected to help the less gifted. On the other hand, mutual criticism is introduced, even in the early school years. Children are first taught to criticize each other, later to anticipate group criticism with self-evaluation [p. 34].

Rollins briefly alluded to manipulative behavior that she felt might be integral to the heavy bureaucratic apparatus in the U.S.S.R., but she provided no extended consideration of this, mentioning the likelihood in only speculative fashion.

Bronfenbrenner (1972) presented several hundred Russian and Swiss children with international school experience with hypothetical situations—21 moral dilemmas—in which a friend or comrade of the child had undertaken varying negative acts ranging from the mild "disorderly eating" to the more serious "theft." The child could either: (*a*) tell an adult; (*b*) tell the other children; (*c*) remonstrate with the friend; or (*d*) refuse to become involved. One might expect that the Russian children, raised in the Soviet collective philosophy, might show more commitment and involvement than the Swiss who, while having had similar group schooling, and thus representing an ideal contrast group, nonetheless were products of a capitalistic social system. Interesting too were the responses of the teachers when asked before measures were taken which option they hoped to get from their children. The Russian teachers hoped the child would take the initiative to correct his comrade, only turning to authority when this failed, a response we might anticipate from Rollins' observations (1972). The Swiss teachers were divided between this option and others.

In 75% of the answers given, the Russian children said they would personally speak with the offending friend, a result obtained with only 33% of the Swiss children. On the other hand, 39% of the Swiss opted for informing an adult, to 11% of the Russian children. Twelve percent of the Russian against 6% of the Swiss would seek the help of a comrade in an offense of violence against another child or disrespect to a teacher. Perhaps of greatest interest were differences to the fourth option: "Do nothing since it didn't concern me." Twenty percent of the Swiss children used this option against 1% of the Russian. All of these differences are statistically significant.

To the extent that children labeled psychopathic frequently behave in ways precisely at issue in Bronfenbrenner's questionnaire, the Russian children did show more sense of personal involvement in contravening the undesirable behavior of a comrade. This is not to argue that the Russian children would necessarily be more effective (although this might be suggested by the 20% of the Swiss who would do nothing) in reducing or eliminating this "antisocial behavior" among themselves. But at least the trespassing occurs in a social climate where a sense of empathy held at the level of the act may well serve a counteractive purpose not served by invoking authority from above. Thus the "guilty" one is, in a sense, working against his comrades rather than defying authority above, which is a more abstracted force, and one from which it is easier to alienate oneself and hence relate to in manipulative fashion.

Bronfenbrenner (1970) reported a similarly interesting set of results involving American and Russian children concerning the relative effects of peer versus adult pressure on antisocial behavior. He took fifth-grade Moscow children from both boarding ($N = 188$) and day schools ($N = 165$) and compared them with an American sample of the same age. The latter were upstate New York public school children, age 12. The conditions of the study put the children in a hypothetical setting where "antisocial behavior" was possible, not unlike the Swiss–Russian study. An example had the children finding a sheet of paper lost by the teacher and containing the answers to a test scheduled for the next day. The friends of our subject child suggest not telling the teacher of the find. The child then has the option either to go along with or go against the group of friends and tell the teacher. Possibilities given the child were that: (a) no one sees his or her response; (b) parents learn of his or her response; (c) peers learn of the response. There were 30 such hypothetical dilemmas in the test. Bronfenbrenner predicted that the Russian children would be less likely to conform to the peer group antisocial behavior than would the American children. A rationale given for his hypothesis was that one reason for Soviet educators to introduce the boarding schools originally was to effect character building in prescribed ways.[3]

Results confirmed that all Russian groups were less ready to engage in antisocial behavior than the American children, as predicted, with boarding school children being least likely. When told that classmates

[3]In the Swiss–Russian study the Russian children showed more peer relating than the Swiss, which may seem contradictory to Bronfenbrenner's hypothesis here. However in the earlier study the peer interaction involved seeking a problem solution, not of, so to speak, creating a problem, i.e., by trespassing as a group on wider cultural norms.

would see their answers, American pupils indicated even greater readiness to engage in socially disapproved behaviors; Soviet children increased their commitment to adult standards. Overall the Russian children showed no distinct tendency to be more influenced by either peers or adults seeing their responses. In summary, Bronfenbrenner distinguished the two groups on the basis that Russian children conform more to the norms of the larger society, American children more to peer pressure:

> Russian children, whether in boarding schools or day schools, are substantially less ready to engage in antisocial behavior when tempted by peers than their American age-mates. In both societies, girls gave more socially approved responses than boys, but there was no significant interaction effect of sex × culture, which indicated that the sex difference was no larger in one country than the other [1970, p. 185].

It must be remembered with this research that we have measures of attitude, not behaviors.

Bronfenbrenner poses but leaves open the fundamental question of whether the character of the children will vary with the training or whether they are only showing situational adaptability and would hence change responses as the society changed. Only by transplanting persons from one culture to another and obtaining personality measures, or by studying persons pre and post rapid cultural change (for example, in South Vietnam before and after the war) could an investigator make inroads to this question.

Bronfenbrenner also reported that preliminary analysis of data compared for three other Western lands (Great Britain, Holland, Switzerland) with three Eastern (U.S.S.R., Hungary, Poland) showed consistently higher adult-oriented responses to the 30 dilemmas among the latter group.

Argentine versus United States Temperament

Moving closer to home for comparisons, Diaz-Guerrero (1967) proposed that qualitatively different modes of coping with stress would be found between Spanish-speaking and English-speaking countries of the Americas. He predicted passive, resigned acceptance of life's circumstances would characterize the Argentinian and active, forceful attack on frustration the White North American.

deFundia, Draguns, and Phillips (1971) set out to test this hypothesis. They collected symptom data and diagnoses among patients hospitalized in Buenos Aires and Cordoba, Argentina, for the years 1961–1967, and compared them with U.S. patients (Worcester State Hospital) hospitalized between 1963 and 1966. In the final comparison groups there were 54 diagnostically and socially matched pairs of men and 42 pairs of women from the two cultures. They found "avoidance of others" as a predominant symptom among Argentinian males and added:

> Moreover, the list of symptoms in which Argentines exceed their counterparts in the U.S. is free of aggression contemplated, perceived or expressed [1971, p. 16]. . . . By contrast, North American patients bring to the fore an elaboration of ideational or overt activity that is often aggressively directed either against self or others [p. 17].

Such differences in symptoms as they found led these researchers to argue that epidemiological studies should include symptoms, not just diagnoses, since the same diagnostic categories might represent dramatically different manifestations, as suggested at the beginning of this chapter. Psychopaths are typically high in aggressiveness, which either gains direct expression through exploiting others, or, on some forms of psychoanalytic theory, accounts for the frequent self-betrayal and failure of the psychopath. The researchers end with a plea which could not better represent this writer's argument relating psychopathy to culture:

> The concordance among these bodies (Havighurst *et al.*; Diaz Guerrero) of information strengthens the case for what we would like to call the "caricature theory" of culture's relation to psychopathology. Within this formulation, psychopathological behavior is only seemingly outlandish, senseless and bizarre; what it represents is the culturally shared mode of behavior that is applied in a wrong way, at the wrong place, and at the wrong time [1971, p. 8].

RESEARCH ON PREVALENCE OF THE PERSONALITY DISORDERS

As the situation currently exists the researcher must be content to accept statistics that include the entire range of Personality Disorders (PD), with the psychopath frequently obscured among them. Epidemiological research has been generally meager even regarding the Personality Disorders, at least partially because of difficulty of diagnosis. Table 8.2 indicates several studies that have reported on their incidence in selected locations, with data on psychopathy listed separately where offered.

The data of Table 8.2 are arranged on the basis of the percentage—from high to low—of Personality Disorders found in the samples

TABLE 8.2
Personality Disorders as Percentage of Research Samples Diagnosed

Country	Sample size	Sample % 301	Sample % 301.7	Location	Reference
U.S.A.	534	22.5	3.3	New York state	Saenger, 1968
Sweden	2520	18.7		Rural	Essen-Moeller, 1956
Holland	300	16.0	4.3	Five university clinics	Saenger, 1968
Iran	928	11.0		Shiraz	Bash & Bash-Liechti, 1974
Poland	1671	4.63		Plock and Chiechanow	Gnat & Henisz, 1966
Lebanon	2374		1.85	Urban	Katchdourian & Churchill, 1973

gathered. Unfortunately the varied nature of the samples does not permit general cross-comparing.

The U.S. and Holland data are clinic samples. Data from the Dutch university clinics were collected during a study meant to compare American and Dutch diagnostic patterns. The Dutch cases are from the years 1966–1967, the New York cases from 1962–1963. In this study psychopathy was diagnosed separately from the other Personality Disorders. All cases were out-patients over 18 years of age. The percentage of psychopaths registered in the two cultures do not differ markedly. The U.S. figure is a mean ($\overline{X}$) value from 6 relatively urban clinics and 18 more rural ones. There were more psychopaths registered in the rural (4.5%) than urban (2.1%) clinics, as well as more Personality Disorders (24.5% to 20.4%). These figures would seem to be based on too few cases to permit much generalizing, and involve only persons in treatment. One might speculate that manipulative, aggressive "con man" behaviors may go more unnoticed or even be condoned in urban settings, whereas they are highly disruptive and visible in more rural settings, which would help account for the greater percentage diagnosed at the latter location.

The data from Iran represent a randomized 1% of 64,386 households from the single city of Shiraz, excluding children under age 6. From these households 2961 cases were screened and 928 selected for diagnosing. Of these the researchers labeled 154 as showing some relevant degree of psychiatric disorder. The researchers stated that while they used the diagnosis of psychopathy "parsimoniously," they did not confine it to sociopathy as per American usage.

The Lebanese data were urban cases collected for comparing with the New Haven data of Hollingshead and Redlich (1958), and in the main comprised data for comparing psychotic versus nonpsychotic disorders. As in the American sample, there was an inverse relation between rate of psychopathy and social class level. Based on the rate of cases per 100,000 population the lower class had 63, middle class 11, and upper class 4. The authors say the sociopathic disorder accounted for about 80% of the Personality Disorders and were treated separately. The 1.85% of sample figure represents a combining of the percentages from the three classes: upper, lower, and middle.

The Swedish data are the oldest reported here, having been collected in 1947, but are exceptionally complete in that only 30 of 2550 cases in this rural setting escaped the interviewing net of the researchers. The figure 18.7% represents, as do the other data in this table, the combined male and female percentage of Personality Disorders diagnosed. It is based on adults only and concerned cases diagnosed as having a minor personality deviation, "minor" being defined by Essen-Moeller as recognizable by doctors and psychiatrists. A "major deviation" was defined as recognizable by "discerning laymen" and included only 5.6% of the sample. Personality Disorders included (a) aggressive, irritable; (b) restless; (c) indolent; and (d) cranks.

The Polish figures cannot be reported with any confidence because only 3 cases of Personality Disorder were diagnosed from the combined sample of the two cities of Plock and Ciechanow. The researchers themselves felt the method of case identification was not adequate to assess psychopathy. The sample was taken in 1961 and was a first effort at a comprehensive psychiatric census in Poland. Purpose of the study was to examine the prevalence of mental disorders contrasting rapidly industrialized Plock (625 random cases, ages 25–29), and more pastoral Ciechanow (1096 random cases, ages 18–59). The only significant difference between them involved the heavier use of alcohol in Plock. The percentage, adjusted for sample size, represents the combined figure for both cities.

NATIONAL INCIDENCE FIGURES ON PSYCHOPATHY AND THE PERSONALITY DISORDERS

Table 8.3 represents a summary of data on incidence of the Antisocial Personality and the Personality Disorders in general that I have put together from various sources. Even disregarding such technical prob-

TABLE 8.3

Comparative Figures for Ten Countries for the Diagnoses Personality Disorders (301) and Antisocial Personality (301.7)

A	B	C	D	E		F	G	
				Diagnosis		PD/AP	PD/AP per 100,000 population	
	Report	Popu-	Total patients			percentage		
Country	year	lation[a]	reported	301	301.7	of patients	PD	AP
Bulgaria	1972	8,6	123,217	3,670		2.98	42.7	
England–Wales	1971	49,0	176,028	16,417		9.33	33.5	
Czecho-slovakia	1972	14,5	30,655	2,087		6.81	14.4	
Canada	1971	27,8 (1972)	56,444[b]		3,871	6.86		13.9
U.S.A.	1974	211,0	434,345[c]	24,728		5.69	11.8	
Finland	1968	4,7 (1969)	12,885[b]		536	4.16		11.4
France	1971	52,5	113,984	5,151		4.52	9.8	
Norway	1972	3,9 (1971)	3,452[b]		148	4.28		0.4
D.D.R.	1973	16,9	126,892[d]	17,947[e]		14.14	106.2	
Denmark	1972	5,0	20,414	3,079[f]		15.08	61.6	

[a] Column in millions to nearest 100,000.
[b] First admissions figure only.
[c] Admissions within the year (including readmissions).
[d] Discharges within the year.
[e] Includes Sexual Deviations (302) and 304–309.
[f] Includes Sexual Deviations (302).

lems as differing mental health practices and differing strategies of reporting data, the figures do not give much basis for meaningful national comparisons. Perhaps their very insufficiency, which extends to other diagnoses as well, will serve to encourage authorities to achieve a more uniform method of data reporting. Cooper, for example, argues that because mental hospital populations offer such a serious source of bias, reports would be better based on community incidence, a point with which I am in full accord. Such studies are, however, immensely demanding of time and resources.

Most countries report Personality Disorders without breaking down incidence figures for the specific varieties. The countries of Table 8.3 are ordered from high to low on the basis of the number of Personality Disorders per 100,000 population. When the year of population estimate differs from the reporting year, the year used for the latter is noted in parentheses (column C).

The raw figures for the D.D.R. (Federal Republic of Germany) are likely to be significantly inflated due to that country's method of reporting (Casper, Dahm, Giersdorf, Rothe, & Schuler, 1975). Their totals are based on the number of patients discharged in a year, and may include the same patient if he were readmitted and again discharged within the same year, a not unexpected occurrence among the Personality Disorders. The D.D.R. figures were not significantly different for the sexes. In interesting contrast to the United States, however, where males significantly predominated, there were slightly more women than men represented in this diagnostic category (9115 to 8832).

The percentage of all cases registered as Personality Disorders in 1973 in the D.D.R. was a rather substantial 14.14% to the United States' 5.69%. This U.S. figure does include both admissions and readmissions, and therefore would permit some measure of comparison with the D.D.R. However the East German figures include also diagnoses 302 and 304–309, which would considerably inflate their figure.

The figure of 126,892 total discharges within the year is also a substantially higher percentage of the total East German population (.0075), than the U.S. admission figures (.0021) for the same year. While only approximately comparable, this difference may be partially attributed to less emphasis on inpatient treatment in the U.S. over the last decade or so. The drop in U.S. state and county mental patients has paralleled the rise of the community mental health movement, with resident patients cresting in 1955 and declining thereafter to a figure less than half that of the peak year. At the same time, the U.S. population itself has risen substantially.

Another factor in addition to problems of reporting technique to consider in comparing countries of Table 8.3 is that many cases, for example in America, are treated privately or in smaller city hospitals and so do not come on the national rolls at all, whereas every East German citizen is in national health care. Still, while the rate for schizophrenia is comparable (which suggests the U.S. has more such cases for the reason of private treatment cited), the raw number of Personality Disorders reported is nearly as large in the D.D.R. report as in the American. Potential comparison is made difficult because the D.D.R. figure, as mentioned, is inflated through inclusion of sexual deviations (302) and diagnoses 304–309.

There was a slight rise in the U.S. state and county mental hospital yearly admissions figures, from 367,963 in 1969 to 434,345 in 1974, but a decline in the Personality Disorders admissions from 27,316 to 24,728. There has also been a substantial decline in number of resident Personality Disorders. In the peak state and county mental hospital population year of 1955, there were 8552 resident cases. The highest year for Personality Disorders was 1964 with 11,280 cases, but this had declined to 9928 by 1968, and to 5813 by 1974.[4] At the same time the total U.S. population had risen considerably between these years, by roughly seven million. Since the diagnosis 301.7 generally represents a substantial part of the 301 total, it can be argued that this diagnosis in America is increasingly less in evidence than at an earlier time. Within this context it is interesting that some social commentators feel the true incidence of this behavior in the United States population at large is on the increase (cf. Harrington, 1974; Mailer, 1957). These latter estimates are, to say the very least, informal, but if the numbers of *psychopathic-like* behaviors are at all increasing, but are appearing less on public hospital rolls, one may wonder if the society is indeed currently less sensitive to such individuals than formerly. Such a speculation can be entertained but not easily confirmed. It does not seem likely, however, that the private hospitals are suddenly accounting for those no longer diagnosed in public institutions.

All *first admission* figures of Table 8.3 are likely to underrepresent the numbers of Personality Disorders reported because they do not include accumulated cases nor readmissions. Hence the Personality Disorders per 100,000 can be taken to be an undercalculation for Canada, Norway, and Finland. Cooper (1966) has reported a rough figure of 5% Personality Disorders for first admissions to mental hospitals in England and Wales (48,266 cases, 1957). American data for 1969 included a total admissions figure of 27,316 Personality Disorders with 10,089 of these being readmissions. Extrapolating this *as if* the percentage of readmissions applied to Canada, Norway, and Finland, their figures in column G of Table 8.3 would rise to 19.1 for Canada, 15.6 for Finland, and .5 for Norway—in each case for the Antisocial Personality alone.

The Bulgarian data, although listed as simply "psychopaths" in the report of health statistics from that country, probably include other Personality Disorders, since I was unable to find these listed elsewhere in their report.

---

[4]While estimated total state and county mental hospital additions continued a slight decline in 1975, to 433,529 cases, as did Personality Disorder additions, to 24,063, the total number of resident patients dipped a remarkable 56% to 191,395. Personality Disorders fell by 24% to 4454. This overall precipitous decline in residence with minimal decline in cases processed suggests a sharply altered treatment strategy.

Because Denmark and the D.D.R. data include sexual deviations (and the D.D.R. 304–309 also), it necessarily inflates the statistics of columns F and G, and therefore these countries are listed apart.

The most meaningful of these generally contaminated data would seem to be those of Bulgaria, England/Wales, Czechoslovakia, the United States, and France. Because the entries in Table 8.3 are based on such discrepant material, a statistical search for trends in the data is precluded, and, of necessity, so are any significant conclusions about the relative incidence of psychopathy in the societies listed. More definitive cross-cultural comparisons await more definitive cross-cultural practices.

9

Psychopathy and the Future

World War II, an unintentional but seemingly consistent breakpoint[1] for much of the present analysis, also served as a milestone in the gathering together of philosophic threads collectively known as existentialism. The pain and misery of existence under wartime oppression, the seeming failure of technology to resolve the fundamental problem of human-to-human relations, and the act of war itself all served to bring European thinkers such as Sartre, Camus, and Jaspers to bitterly challenge traditional philosophies of reason. It is not that the philosophies were new; Kierkegaard was published in the 1840s and Husserl was active at the turn of the century. The ideas seemed rather to come to urgent focus in an historical period when technology appeared capable for the fist time of destroying those very beings who had created and perfected it. The era of atomic power brought with it the realization that man could so mishandle himself and his brothers—through the very reasoning ability that set him apart from the creature world—that it was deemed crucial to go back to fundamental philosophic questions of the

---

[1]Nixon (1970) has made a similar judgment about the importance of this conflict in discussing the limits of capitalism in promoting human welfare. In his eyes the "establishment" has had control of U.S. national policy since the war, and has had little serious challenge from left or right. Compare also Albee (1977); Mailer (1957). Erich Fromm's trenchant observations on America are also post-war.

nature of Being and the meaning of existence in the face of technology's steady march to apparent domination of man.

Reason, particularly as seen in the progressive social–industrial order, was the root of the value system brought into question by the existentialists. The values taken for granted by this rational–industrial order—the mastering of nature; acquiring, producing and consuming goods; and striving for material wealth—all came under growing attack. Reason showed its potential unreason in such absurdities as, e.g., increasingly inert bureaucracies and the seeming disregard for human feeling consequent on their growth.

Knowledge may not only reach absurd heights in cold and unfeeling translation to social policy, it is perforce limited and incomplete, even at molecular levels, as Heisenberg and Goedel have shown in the realms of physics and mathematics. At its most fundamental level nature is an open, indeterminate system, say existentialists, intrinsically resistant to precise deduction from self-evident premises. Without the possibility of inevitable certainty even in the material world, man is necessarily thrown back on his own individual, personal decisions in relating to his fellow man and the world about. "Philosophers of despair" such as Kierkegaard and writers such as Camus, Sartre, and Rilke were widely read in this early post-World War II period, their ideas aired and emulated by the New Bohemians from Saint-Germain-des-Pres to North Beach, San Francisco. The hero of reason who "came, saw, and conquered" a situation in orderly, determinate fashion—whether in nature or in society—began giving way in popular philosophy as well as in art to Camus' stranger, and the anti-hero whose ultimate survival turns out to be threatened by the irrationality of those who would force conventional "rational" values on him, regardless of his fitness for convention. In the case of Camus' Meursault there was the lack of grief at the death of his mother, a convention demanded by society regardless of how potentially farcical in any given mother–son relation: a clarion call to which the most knavish are expected to respond. Meursault failed this test and on the pretext of having killed a man, absurdly, is condemned to the guillotine:

> Is my client on trial for having buried his mother, or for killing a man? he asked. There were some titters in court. But then the Prosecutor sprang to his feet and, draping his gown round him, said he was annoyed at his friend's ingeniousness in failing to see that between these two elements of the case there was a vital link. They hung together psychologically, if he might put it so [Camus, 1960, pp. 121–122].[2,3]

[2] Reprinted by permission of Alfred A. Knopf, Inc. from Albert Camus, *The Stranger,* © 1960 by Alfred A. Knopf, Inc. translated by Stewart Gilbert.

[3] Duff (1977), in an essay about psychopathy and moral understanding, accuses this same Meursault of psychopathy because he seems unable to understand or take part in the values, interests, and emotions of those around him. While I would agree that Meursault seems unencumbered by "civilized values," his seeming inability to place the values of

Not to worship upward mobility, tangible success, physical attractiveness is to set a poor standard for the psychopathically inclined, viewed here as dependent on the intrapsychic constellations, or if one prefers, habit hierarchy, of conventionality, competition, "getting ahead." This is not to argue that the psychopath especially behaves in these traditional ways; he frequently does not, as already abundantly shown. However at some level he subscribes to these conventions, and his successes in manipulating others depend on their subscribing to them as well. Too, while individualism is a hallmark of both "existential man" and the psychopath, its forms are vastly different in the two instances. The individualism of the "existentialist" relates itself precisely to the responsibility of the individual, i.e., responsibility for his decisions, for his very existence. The psychopath is individual only in the sense of rawest ego, of placing himself ahead of everyone else in the most blatant fashion. The psychopath indeed stands behind none of his decisions. He flees instead into inauthenticity—to the shelter of an unreal or superfluous facade (Haefner, 1961) as protection against his fundamental Being. The psychopath is fully estranged from Being existentially conceived; he is paradoxically maximally dependent on others. For him there is no "thou," but many of "them." He is the antithesis of existential man.

The Germanic school of phenomenology, while more austere and abstract than the French existentialisms, has also concerned itself fundamentally with Being (Dasein). While Barrett tells us (1962) that Husserl intended to hue to traditional Cartesian rationalism, the phenomenological method which he employed turned radically away from rationalist premises to the point of questioning the very existence of a rational being. Searching for a "third way" (Barrett, 1962, p. 130) between realism and idealism, he turned to rigorous and descriptive study of what was given in conscious experience. With Husserl's students Heidegger and Jaspers, the focus of research became the analysis of individual being-in-the-world (*Daseinanalyse*). For Heidegger the being-in-the-world is the Being of a self in inseparable relations with a not-self, or world of objects and other selves (Blackham, 1952). Heidegger was particularly distressed by philosophies that ignored the fundamental ontological question of the meaning of Being. Questions concerned with the nature of truth, contemplation of non-Being, and the human sense of dread are important themes in Heidegger's writings and have obvious implications for a psychology meaning to speak to health and ill-health. Could the psychopath, as typically portrayed, realize his Being, ground his existence through coming to grips with death, with non-Being, as Heidegger would require of authentic Being?

Karl Jaspers has been an important contributor to the phe-

---

others means also that he is unable to exploit those others. He cannot even ape conventional values, and thus winds up himself the exploited, the loser.

nomenological–existential tradition as well as a major figure in world psychiatry. For Jaspers *Dasein* or mode of existence is being-in-a-situation. The situation is the concrete and particular circumstances in which man is embedded in his world. It is the zone in which activities are carried out and where empirical being can be promoted or assailed. Also impinging on the person is the mutual action of other agents sharing his field. Jaspers includes then not only contemporaneous forces of the moment, of the immediate situation, but economic and political structures of a society as well. The prevailing outlook of, e.g., science in the culture, and general cultural relations (Collins, 1963) contribute to shaping being-in-a-situation. This altogether Marxian emphasis provides a framework for examining abnormal (or "problem") states of Being in the context of the culture in which the individual is found. Jaspers is, however, critical of the mass man ideals of both capitalism and communism, where decisions are impersonally made on the basis of "all of us" (Collins, 1963, p. 93).

Jaspers has been especially concerned with the depersonalization of man through his being viewed as a mere social unit in a technocracy; there is in the modern age a "spiritual hole" in the human condition. We are winning control of the environment, but are not, while inappropriately employing the same tactics, profiting man. There is a loss of the communal sense in modern technocracies. There are mass organizations to be sure, but they tend to propagandize for the state in the form of national and class pride. In a sense, the technocratic state takes care of empirical, everyday-living being, but not to the needs of the human spirit—of spiritual being.

It is within these perspectives of human hollowness and cultural press that one can view the peculiar predicament of the psychopath. Myriad theorists have judged him a hollow shell—recall Cleckley or Gough, from quite distinct traditions. Tuned to the world around—one of Eysenck's extraverts—the psychopath may be viewed existentially as suffering from "an illness of Being." He is inauthentic in an existential sense. His self is restricted to empirical being where what is regarded as real is confined to those things that are objects for it, determined in consciousness. He is in the realm of "being there," as Jaspers might have said, an objectively determined thing, not in the realm of "being oneself," the realm of choice and decision transcending the empirical world (Blackham, 1952). This objective, everyday world cannot, however, shut out human situations which have pertinence for transcendent or spiritual being. Such situations bring man to realization of his mortality, and at the same time his existence; they bring him to the "metaphysical search" for meaning, spirit, the transcendent (Collins,

1963). The psychopathically inclined seem particularly "crippled Beings" when it comes to these critical but freeing realizations; psychopaths epitomize the inauthentic because they are fixated on the object world.

EXISTENTIAL MAN AND PSYCHOPATHY

Haefner (1961) has produced a monograph which, following to some extent the work of Jaspers, and particularly Binswanger, analyzes the nature of psychopathy from the phenomenological–existential standpoint. He presents three case histories that are treated in careful detail: one a *"hochstaplerischer Betrueger"* ("conman"), one with hypochondriacal symptoms, and the third of "labile mood."

With psychopathy, Haefner believes, there is a failure of development of what he calls the "existential conscience." It is this conscience that plays a decisive role in the possibility for a completion of Being, that is, a uniting of the various aspects of Being. The demand on the person in the general society is to give up some of his own egocentric desires in favor of communal demands. In the psychopath, however, this socially facilitative conscience remains stunted, covered up. He is unable to recognize the rights of others in a communal sense; he has failed to develop his own "being with others" (*Mitsein*). Because of this he is unable to truly "be" himself—to exist fully.

The need to accommodate to the social order, to develop social Being, may be experienced as a threat to the would-be psychopath's own "self power" even as a child. This is power as dominating, as egoistic. However this primitive, uncompromising egoism brings with it the inability to realize limits to the self, such as one's personal finiteness, instead there is loss of Being in unreal, inauthentic possibilities (*weglose uneigentlicher Moeglichkeiten*). I take Kallwas to be referring back to Jasper's restricted empirical Being and the position that the psychopath is severely limited to this sphere. The communal world (*Mitwelt*) insofar as it is experienced by the psychopath is seriously narrowed and limited, which in turn limits the extent to which Being in its various possibilities can develop.

This now cut off, stunted self is denied the normal pleasures of human community in spite of typically frantic efforts at such attainment, seen for example in the extreme sociability of the psychopath —an "inauthentic possibility." To bridge this gap between stunted Being and a realm of unreal, unbounded wishfulness, and to attain some (albeit distorted) sense of unity of Being, a facade is erected.

The facade functions to conceal true Being and thereby hides any authenticity in self and in relations with others. Full awareness is denied in a sort of "existential dissociation" and blocked desires might show themselves in caricature of the true needs were the person more "fully human." Thus in the case of Kallwas' confidence man, there is a facade of unwarranted optimism; in the hypochondriacal symptoms, there is a distortion of the need for warmth from one's fellow humans distorted into the need for physical "warming" of the cold body. In the labile man it led to an overfantasized and overvalued view of reality. The facade promises a wellbeing, a set of possibilities regarding unfulfilled needs resulting from failed self-realization. It provides a unitary if one-sided life style in which blocked desires are carried out in distorted fashion. The schism between what might be called fantastic possibilities and the truncated self is never fully bridged in a way to create a true unity of Being. Instead the inauthentic and distorted unity of the facade becomes the psychopath's reality.

The emphasis of Haefner's existential analysis concerns the inner experiences of the psychopath as she/he attempts to master the lived environment. The facade is a sort of "character armor," or more broadly, "living style" erected to deal with the split between truncated Being and the "wide world of infinite possibilities." Unfortunately for us the three case histories he offers are German in origin, and seriously dated (patients born before World War I), and while nicely detailed, they permit no easy comparison with contemporary American experience and examples. One would be interested for example in the variation if any in the structure of the facade—that is to say, its elements as they might differ one culture to another. Also the need itself for such a structure would likely vary depending on how strongly a culture detained a man from attending to his realization of Being. In this regard, remember that Jaspers took a dim view of cultures producing "mass man."

Even so, Haefner's emphasis is more descriptive and dynamic than genetic or social. It is the latter aspects, e.g., how does the culture contribute to the nature and structure of the facade, which if specificable, would permit us to round out a picture of the nature and extent of psychopathic cases. For example Haefner's con man Daniel Fuerst experienced immense freedom from his mother but strictness and rejection from his father, unless he constantly agreed with father. Haefner saw this inconsistency as the basis of the splitting of Being for Daniel between friendly, open freedom on one side and stubborn, narrow boundaries on the other. The Being of the child is not capable of holding such a contradictory world together, in Haefner's view. To bring unity to this split, Daniel followed his mother's lead in allowing the father to think everything at home went his way. Daniel built a facade of the model child of apparent happy optimism, inauthentic though it was. The reader will recognize this family portrait as one of the common types Buss (1966) has associated with psychopathy. There is unfortunately little consideration in Haefner of the broader cultural input to the system.

Perhaps an outwardly oriented marketing culture requires more facade construction and more inauthenticity than those in which the *"Mitsein"* plays a more central and critical role. Or perhaps any facade erected where image is praised is less disturbing to the culture as a whole, is more expected, and hence acceptable. This would seem inevitably to follow from the meaning of image. It gives a mere appearance of reality, hence is inevitably inauthentic, a reflection of what is imaged. It is a momentary "snapshot" of Being, purely empirical, helping us to hide from subjective, spiritual being.

THE PSYCHOPATH AND THE COUNTERCULTURE

Just as much of this analysis of psychopathy and the American milieu has marked the era of World War II as significant for American cultural change, so experiences related to the American war in Vietnam have given rise to interesting cultural counter currents. At least ostensibly they have been largely antithetical to those that have here been seen as hitherto modal to the culture. Disillusioned with bigness, with materialism, with rationality displayed through technology—led by students faced with a draft call to a remote war which seemed not to correspond with its declared dimensions and purpose—Americans were not insignificantly shaken in their public confidence in familiar institutions and accepted practices. The story by now has been told and retold to the point of becoming cant, so that yet another telling is superfluous. Suffice it to say that beginning roughly in the middle 1960s there was a gradually rising crescendo of opposition to much established American power and tradition. Impertinent questions hacking at the very foundation of American self-consciousness—ranging from freedom of speech to property ownership—were broached, debated, physically fought over. At the same time a black woman in Alabama elected not to sit in the back of a public bus as prescribed, and the ensuing strife touched off a swell of civil rights activism for minorities in America. Even unconcerned or neutral majority whites found themselves uneasy at the cleft between promises made each citizen regarding freedom and equality and what occurred when these legal rights were demanded.

Not only was national morality regarding the central government and basic institutions put on trial, but public morality was questioned and sharp demand for change flooded many areas of endeavor that heretofore were seemingly untouchable, i.e., the academies, the arts, science itself—the very language one spoke and had seemingly always spoken. An era of rejection of vested authority, especially authority standing on the precedents of age, wealth, and social position, came into vogue. Such authority was sorely tried and occasionally toppled, e.g., the military draft. Though deplored by those in dominant positions, the waves of change had gathered powerful momentum and swept through, around and over institutions that formerly seemed impregnable. This was widely heralded—even by numerous "old guard" who clasped the new egalitarianism in passionate embrace (see Reich, 1971, for a popular example).

As suggested, these changes were meant to uproot and displace many of those values herein judged intrinsic to American modal personality, and which served nicely to encourage psychopathically related behaviors. Thus ruthless competition and materially defined success were criticized and satirized, and communal living and "dropping out" of competition became something of a fashion among subgroups of young Americans. Searching for development of internal peace rather than external signs of the good life was evident in the turn toward mystical religions and meditation, with a consequent rejection of established Western faiths thought to have become too "fat," too worldly. Jeans, the working clothes of the farmer, worn by youth as rejection of formal "upper class" attire, became a symbol of rejection of class distinctions in general.

In psychotherapy, group therapy, with its more democratic spirit, immediate reality testing, and less exclusive prices than individual therapy, became increasingly the therapy of choice. Within its borders, "encountering" erupted in which participants were challenged to relate "honestly" to one another and to eschew social titles, roles, and other masks believed to associate with manipulation of others in castelike relationships. Overt concern for interpersonal relationships struck a new high in the United States (cf. Rogers, 1970). Prodded by theorists like Maslow, May, and Rogers, a search for more authentic experience became manifested. Even that bulwark of American cultural values, the institution of business itself, starting with the National Training Laboratory at Mt. Bethel, Maine, and evidenced in the recent work of Argyris

(1969, 1975), came under attack in its traditional form. Business leaders themselves were often dissatisfied with the corporate world. Attempts are being made to change American business from the top, training management to hold more humanistic goals, to moderate the profit motive. The corporation or company is being recognized as a system in which the weakest link, i.e., the workers, could bring down the whole if not treated carefully. The corporate giants, according to the "new morality," should take concern for their total environment, including the land and sky from which they pull raw materials. In a recent interview, Bendix Corporation's Werner Blumenthal asked rhetorically: "Which comes first, the profit or the people?" The interviewer then noted that: "Costs, of course, are not irrelevant to Bendix." Then Blumenthal again: "But the market economy, like democracy itself, is based on a moral perception: that people are more than a means to an end [Perry, 1977, p. 5]."

In psychological theory a counterforce in the coalescence of the humanist movement became visible and active in this same "Vietnam decade." Their credo is fittingly described by a layman:

> When the Association for Humanistic Psychology sent word that it was meeting here . . . I saw a chance to explore humanism, for this philosophy seems to be a crescendo of the future. Signs of this new wave have been emerging for a decade: it may be, as one speaker here said, that this conference represents the eve of revolution. Bits and pieces of the humanist pattern include Zen; yoga; transcendental meditation; transactional analysis; concern for the dying; civil rights for all persons; making ethical concerns a part of medical-school curricula; open classrooms; the American Lutheran Church's sponsorship of the University of Minnesota medical school's program in human sexuality, whose goal is to reunite the body and the mind in one whole person; admission of women to the ministry; food co-operatives; gay liberation; child-free marriages; the Equal Rights Amendment; affirmative action for women in jobs; Ralph Nader's consumerism; organic foods; vegetarianism; and the ombudsman concept [Hacker, 1975, p. 29].

Here is a catalogue of "pros" with which a communally oriented commentator would hardly dare to quarrel.

I have suggested elsewhere (Smith, 1973) that could the core of humanistic values come to fruition, the psychopath as a major behavioral problem might disappear, or at any rate show recessive qualities in later generations (which is not to deny that other human social diseases might arise to take its place, as heart disease or cancer now rises up to strike down those who might in earlier generations have been victims of tuberculosis or scarlet fever). Only from the perspective of the rawest organicist would it be possible even to imagine a "mental problem" free future for man. Failing this brittle utopianism, one might still wonder how the traditional symptoms of psychopathy have been viewed in the decade since the "new consciousness" urgently broke in America.

CONTRASTING VIEWS OF
THE COUNTERCULTURE

In Cleckley's most recent edition of his *Mask of Sanity*, he evinces a strongly negative view of the countercultural forces discussed above, treating this movement largely from writer Alan Harrington's perspective. Harrington's recent book, *Psychopaths* (1974), in which he takes a fearsome look at the psychopath as the man for the future, served as the main stimulus for Cleckley's ire. Harrington's jarring thesis first appeared in the popular magazine *Playboy* and prompted the rejoinder:

> Some of the people quoted or cited by this author of the *Playboy* article (and the subsequent book) seem to be spokesmen for, or prominent figures in, the recent movement of rebellion often referred to as the *counterculture*. In this movement we find zealots who embrace hallucinatory confusion under the influence of potentially brain-damaging psychedelic drugs and aggressively proclaim it as a religious experience. Here, too, we find the antihero, often a figure flaunting treason and dishonor along with his unkept beard, bare-footedness, and defiantly frayed blue jeans. In this so-called *counterculture* the *antihero* was not only welcomed but by some virtually enshrined. It has been fashionable also in this movement to degrade the high passion and glory of sexual love to a significance not far from that of a belch. Perhaps, in this general and heedless effort to reverse the basic values, almost anything traditionally regarded as undesirable, or despicable, might be automatically stamped with the sign of approval [Cleckley, 1976, p. 235].

In reality, however, Harrington's thesis has little to do with these byproducts of the rejection of traditional values. On the contrary he reverts back to the older ethic against which countercultural motifs were quite precisely aimed. Although ostensibly representing the man of tomorrow, Harrington's sensationalized account is more in keeping with the American of yesterday. Cleckley rightly responds indignantly to the call for us to adopt the predatory life style, vaunted by Harrington as the healthiest mode of response to human futures. Portraying a rogues' gallery of horrors, Harrington wonders if all of us shouldn't throw down our *Mitsein* and join in "acting out":

> No more meditation, musing over this doubt and that fear. No more plodding in earnest pursuit of a sober and responsible life plan. For the psychopath, and now his followers, this is a fool's game. Instead, for them, physically, spiritually, travel, move, make out, exploit, strike back, enjoy, unimpeded by any guilt whatever, compassionate only when aesthetically excited or on whim, cross all borders, made new after each illegal crossing, keep going [1974, p. 271].

Cleckley focuses on Harrington's most extreme argument, and in my judgment correctly sees sophistry in Harrington's rhetorical question as to whether or not we should all become psychopaths in order to survive. Cleckley's answer is that if Harrington truly understood psychopathy he would lay no such claim. He does this from his familiar position that the psychopath is insane in the sickness sense of this term. In this context, therefore, it would be as if Harrington asked if healthy, one should want to be literally ill, which very likely is a sophistical question, though not from Harrington's perspective, for he sees the psychopathic life style as "the new health."

Harrington is in tune with the thesis here presented to the extent of viewing the psychopathic style as more the rule than the exception in American society. Unlike him, however, I do not see this style as a "hope for the future." For Harrington asks his reader to join the crippled, existentially inhuman examples of a culture not necessarily healthy in its emphases: All appear demonstrably tied to empirical being in the crassest sense. At the most conservative one could read Harrington as providing a sensational warning against psychopathic trends. While such possibilities undeniably exist, they would match those American values displayed here as traditional, even when played out in the "hippie scene" so apathetically viewed by Cleckley. While Harrington's "new man" may have fastened on new *ends*, e.g., having "fun" instead of a steady job, the *means* are the same familiar catalogue of exploitation. Indeed, Norman Mailer, from whose essay *The White Negro* (1957) Harrington has taken many cues, ties psychopathy to an exclusively male search for bigger and better orgasm. The 1950s "hipster" so idealized by Mailer is defined in ways which indicate how tied he is to traditional values: As an exploited black in a white civilization he receives no "cultural nectar [1957, p. 9]" because he is at the "alienated bottom of exploitable human material [p. 9]." The response of the hipster is to become a "sexual outlaw." Marx has made the same point, i.e., the enjoyments of the worker, even while rising, do not keep pace with those of the capitalist, which may be inaccessible to the working man (Marx, 1970). Marx's solution would be to change the society, not "try to go it one better" by recommending one "out selfish" his or her neighbor.

Harrington's effort falls short as well in haphazardly mixing clearly nonpsychopathic examples, e.g., a seemingly schizophrenically disturbed 16-year-old murderer, with more appropriate cases. Cleckley (1976), whose own diagnostic criteria are widely known and commonly employed, fails to point out Harrington's seriously flawed lumping of cases under the rubric psychopathy. On the face of it this confusion of cases may not seem serious, but it distorts Harrington's entire argument in railing against countercultural values. A case in point is his discussion of the radical social activist, Jerry Rubin. Harrington attempts to bring Rubin and his unorthodox ways of attacking traditional American values under the psychopathic motif, and in so doing fails to consider the underlying morality of Rubin's attack. In fascination with the style, he seems to have missed the substance. The very violence of Rubin's attack suggests the frustration and anger of the moralist, of one who would shake America out of its immoral behavior in Vietnam and the American southland. Such a posture is manifestly *not* psychopathic according to most diagnosticians.[4] Harrington's analysis may be unduly influenced by the hard-sell personality marketing that previously has been remarked as a cultural demand. That is, if one wants to be noticed by the news hucksters it is deemed necessary to behave excessively—to appeal to the news market in order to be heard. Thus Rubin dressed himself as a caricature of Uncle Sam in order to get a media hearing for social criticism. Perhaps even a moralist is obliged to adopt the tactics that fit the milieu with which he is confronted. Psychopathic? I think not.

Harrington misreads the counterculture as the dog-eat-dog world of familiar nineteenth-century predation. This is not to say that countercultural ideals are not corruptible into something approaching such competitive mores; jeans have long since become an expensive fashion garment. But that is surely not the sense and substance of the movement nor the view one achieves from examining the behaviors of those imbued with its precepts, for example the humanist movement discussed earlier. In recently responding to the argument that implementation of countercultural ideals might truly result in the extinction of the psychopath, an editorial reviewer expressed his doubt that such would occur. Commenting on the manuscript of Smith (1973) he noted

> Insofar as it has to do with *psychotherapy*, a suggestion is proferred that if our culture were to evolve into the Argyris "B" type of value system, based on interpersonal feelings rather than intellectualized solutions, on peer-openness rather than parent-child one-upmanship and power displays, etc., the psychopathic phenomenon "might not" (in theory) evolve??? I enjoyed the paper right up to this point, which was really "reaching" and highly dubious. The author has every right to make his own theoretical speculations clear in this fashion, but I was just thinking how beautifully I observed one of the "most" psychopathic guys I ever knew "operate"— and he did so via the T-group philosophy known as "B" . . . so, this suggestion clearly turned me off [personal communication, 1972].

---

[4]One could argue that Rubin were psychopathic if he now embraced those morals/ethics that he previously attacked, as has been rumored. But I know of no evidence that he has done so.

The reviewer's experience regarding encounter groups is a not un-known occurrence, is probably not even rare.

Indeed leaders of "growth groups" themselves have impressed observers as playing by traditional societal rules. Shepard (1975) observed in his biography of Frederick Perls that the following criticisms fit his subject: Indulgent of self, wanted to be on stage all the time, maintained uninvolvement with patients via the workshop method of case presentation, competed with other men, and was therapeutically easier on women than men, especially if the ladies were attractive. Shepard, however, found these criticisms rather positive because "Fritz set a standard that others might well adopt. His 'indulgence' can be seen as a shameless commitment to do that which pleased *him* not *others* [p. 215, italics in original]."

The occasional naivete seen among "reflex liberals" imbued with doctrinaire social science mores makes them an obvious target for psychopathic manipulators playing by Harrington's rules, as the case study of "Ron" (Chapter 2) emphasized. Nonetheless, such operators are regressive aberrations from the point of view of the morality of which I write, and not its main spokesmen. They employ the individualistic, egocentric style still widely practiced in exploiting a tentative, uncertain, but perhaps budding alternative.

Harrington's *Psychopaths* (1974) is a curious mixture of solid insights (e.g., on psychopathic styles in highly respected U. S. social circles), confusing diagnoses, and sensationalism, built on traditional American morality and ethics. The entire setting and all examples are American; the author's fears and hopes for the future are American. Even if Harrington were correct in his assessment of the future, his analysis suffers seriously from this one-cultural *Weltanschauung*. That is, it is this Western man of Mafia-like morality who is given to us as the prototype of world man:

> An absolute and continuing need at every moment to acquit oneself with grace under pressure drives this individual. If he scores, triumphs, gets his way, he grows and lives more intensely. If he fails, allows anyone or any circumstance to put him down, he actually dies a little, his energies weaken, and his soul diminishes: he may even sicken and; Mailer believes, contract cancer [1974, p. 24].

Between Harrington and the humanists one finds two distinctly different views of just the American future alone being projected. From Harrington:

> The psychopathic style has become epidemic around the country. . . . The style has infiltrated everywhere. . . . The prevalence of what was once comfortably defined as

deviant behavior has turned the game around. Indeed, the psychopath now pursues, defies, and may be bent on remaking *us*. Whether violent or passive, he seems concerned only with today, and this way of living has grown into a philosophical or even spiritual force that seriously (or laughing) threatens all that we have been taught to believe in [1974, pp. 189–190].

Humanists see no future in Harrington's future:

Humanists acknowledge the risks in change. The alternative though, they say, is disaster: rising crime rates, disintegrating families, and growing social frustration. The solution, say humanists, is to create a society in which individuals can be open, honest, intimate, and authentic. To do this one must let go—of the past, of control, even of the present. This is a vision of a life in which each individual can fulfill his or her full potential, in a way that is loving and creative and not self-destructive or exploitive of others [Hacker, 1975, p. 22].

What these positions have in common despite their antithetical elements is an emphasis on individualism—one benign, the other egocentric. Hogan (1975) has supported my belief that in principle, the counterculture movement represents a repudiation of the traditional cult of individualism. Hogan argues that if the social environment is benign—and I take him here to mean an environment which is not viciously competitive or exploitative—then egocentric behavior displayed there takes on a clearly pathological hue. Deviants in this respect in such a society can be helped if they form attachments to nondeviant groups there:

They must come to regard the continued existence of the group as important. Finally, they must believe that the welfare and continued existence of the group is in some way tied to their actions. . . . A deviant must discover a nondeviant person or set of persons who represent(s) a viable cultural group, whose approval matters to him. Then he must realize that this approval is dependent on his performance in accordance with the standards of the group. To make this quite specific, social deviants must experience a form of irrational or religious conversion to a belief in the standards of an organic and functioning social group or entity [Hogan, 1975, p. 538].

This may sound like the confessions of Arthur Koestler (1961) regarding communistic practice, and such a strategy of creating a feeling of group responsibility is part of the strong emphasis put on clubs and common projects in Eastern lands. The "Free Democratic Youth" (FDJ) of East Germany is such a group. The intent is to bind members to one another and to the broader ideals. This is done through the sort of virtually religious emphasis Hogan argues for above: close intimate contacts, group monitoring of morality, concern for each and every fellow member. We have seen this as well in the Bronfenbrenner (1972) and Rollins (1972) accounts of Soviet educational practice (cf. also Hsian, 1977, on China).

Such group feeling, or at least the promotion of it, must give members a sense of belonging, of purpose, of goal—of something other than the alienated, anomic feelings increasingly common in the West (cf. Meyers, 1976; Smith & Griffith, 1978[5]). While organizations like the East German FDJ may smack of totalitarianism to American ears, they represent in reality nothing greatly different from what the McCords under the rubric milieu therapy recommend for psychopathy, or what Bronfenbrenner hints at for Western youth. The difference, as well as the probability for success, lies once again with the broader cultural fabric of values.

Guttentag (1977), using sociologist Bell's framework of three phases of society—pre-industrial, industrial, and post-industrial—believes the U. S. is entering the third at present, in which the primary social unit is the community organization rather than the individual, and where major decisions will be less controlled by the market and arrived at more through collective negotiations among major interest groups. The post-industrial society centers on human services and requires cooperation and reciprocity rather than the coordinated productivity and hierarchical relations among men prevailing in industrial societies. Although it is not Guttentag's argument, such a change should have profound effects on the personality modes which would emerge to cope with the new communal social order, where we have a "game between persons" (Guttentag, 1977, p. 32) rather than "against nature" (p. 31), or favoring hierarchical relations, in pre-industrial and industrial societies, respectively. Guttentag's allusion to games is unfortunate, but the needs of this post-industrial society, as she states them, may foster personality modes more in keeping with those Belaief, Deutsch, and Argyris (see Chapter 7) project.

United States science too is retreating from its long-standing pretense of "value free" inquiry in a social–political vacuum. As a replacement for the positivistic, cause–effect metaphysic and its accompanying merely descriptive ethics, Western social science commentators are beginning to propose a turn to a dialectic view of man and society (cf. Buss, 1976; Cvetkovich, 1976; Guttentag, 1977; Riegel, 1973; Rychlack,

---

[5]In their previously mentioned study, Smith and Griffith (1978) found the strong correlation of .50 between the MMPI Pd Scale and Elmore's Social Feeling Index, a measure of anomie (Elmore, 1965).

1968). It is not that the ideas are new, as readers of Hegel, Marx, or theorists weighing Freud know, but ideas regarding the dialectical status of man in society have been thrust on the scene as an antidote to the apparent failure of positivistic science to speak to the human condition. In Guttentag's view this means research which is used in program decisions affecting the involved constituents not merely the entrepreneurial scientist (1977, p. 36). There is also increasing recognition that "We should treat people, for scientific purposes, *as if they were human beings,* capable not only of reacting to, but also interacting with and, at times, even changing the environment [Cvetkovich, 1976, p. 1]."

Buss sees the new morality of humanism doomed in the West if it does not go beyond mere notions of changing individuals to an emphasis on changing human institutions. He offers a clarion call which may herald a new philosophy for social science in America:

> Humanistic psychologists should begin to realize that self-actualization, Becoming, and the realization of one's potential is *conditional upon* a certain social reality. Humanistic psychologists should begin to consider the kind of real social conditions which will permit the maximization of individual development, richness of inner experience, expansion of consciousness, etc. Humanistic psychologists should adopt a *radical criticism* of existing dehumanizing social conditions, and thereby help bring into being a humanistic society. Humanistic psychologists should unite their emphasis upon human values with an equal emphasis upon human action in order to realize humanistic values on a large scale. To the extent the above prescriptions are not carried out, humanistic psychology will remain a class psychology—relevant to those who "have" (i.e., achieved sufficient economic wealth) and completely irrelevant to those who are the "have-nots" . . . . At this point in our social evolution we should voluntarily abandon the pursuit of a "humanistic" psychology as it presently exists, that is, as a bourgeois-class psychology for human growth. The establishment of a meaningful and valuable *humanistic* psychology—a psychology which can speak to the self-development of the majority of individuals—is conditional upon a humanistic society [1976, p. 258].[6]

Such a society will be no comfortable home for the games that psychopaths play.

---

[6]Reprinted with permission of S. Karger AG, Basel, from A. R. Buss, Development of dialectics and development of humanistic psychology, *Human Development,* 1976, **19,** 248–260.

References

Abramson, E. E. The counselor as a Machiavellian. *Journal of Clinical Psychology*, 1973, **29,** 348–349.

Adler, A. In H. L. Ansbacher & R. Ansbacher (Eds.), *The individual psychology of Alfred Adler*. New York: Basic Books, 1956.

Albee, G. W. The short, unhappy life of clinical psychology. *Psychology Today,* 1970, **4,** 42–43, & 74.

Albee, G. W. The protestant ethic, sex, and psychotherapy. *American Psychologist,* 1977, **32,** 150–161.

Allport, G. W. *Personality and social encounter*. Boston: Beacon Press, 1960.

American Psychiatric Association. *Diagnostic and statistical manual: Mental disorders.* (1st ed.) Washington, D.C.: American Psychiatric Association, 1952.

American Psychiatric Association. *Diagnostic and statistical manual of mental disorders.* (2nd ed.) Washington, D.C.: American Psychiatric Association, 1968.

Anastasi, A. *Differential psychology*. New York: Macmillan, 1958.

Argyris, C. The incompleteness of social psychological theory: Examples from small group, cognitive consistency, and attitude research. *American Psychologist,* 1969, **24,** 893–908.

Argyris, C. Dangers in applying results from experimental social psychology. *American Psychologist,* 1975, **30,** 469–485.

Arieti, S. *Interpretation of schizophrenia*. New York: Bruner, 1955.

At Bowling Green: News for Alumni. "People," December 5, 1975.

Ax, A. F. Psychophysiological methodology for the study of schizophrenia. In R. Roessler & N. S. Greenfield (Eds.), *Physiological correlates of psychological disorder*. Madison, Wisc.: University of Wisconsin Press, 1962.

Bakan, D. The influence of phrenology on American psychology. *Journal of the History of the Behavioral Sciences,* 1966, **2,** 192–220.

Barrett, W. Introduction to phenomenology and existentialism. In W. Barrett & H. D. Aiken (Eds.), *Philosophy in the twentieth century.* Vol. 3. New York: Random House, 1962.

Bash, K. W., & Bash-Liechti, J. Studies on the epidemiology of neuropsychiatric disorders among the population of the city of Shiraz, Iran. *Social Psychiatry,* 1974, **9,** 163–171.

Belaief, L. Self esteem and human equality. *Philosophy and Phenomenological Research,* 1975, **36,** 25–43.

Bell, R. Q. A reinterpretation of the direction of effects in studies of socialization. *Psychological Review,* 1968, **75,** 81–95.

Bender, L. The concept of pseudopsychopathic schizophrenia in adolescents. *American Journal of Orthopsychiatry,* 1959, **29,** 491–512.

Berg, N. L. Self-concept of neurotic and sociopathic criminal offenders. *Psychological Reports,* 1974, **34,** 622.

Bethlehem, D. W. The effect of westernization on cooperative behavior in Central Africa. *International Journal of Psychology,* 1975, **10,** 119–224.

Biometry Branch, OPPE, National Institute of Mental Health Health Services and Mental Health Administration. *Trends in resident patients state and country mental hospitals, 1950–1968.* Chevy Chase, Md.: National Inst. of Mental Health, 1970.

Bisky, L. *Zur Kritik der buergerlichen Massenkommunikationsforschung.* Berlin: VEB Deutscher Verlag der Wissenschaften, 1976.

Blackham, H. J. *Six existentialist thinkers.* New York: Harper & Row, 1952.

Block, J. H. Conceptions of sex role: some cross-cultural and longitudinal perspectives. *American Psychologist,* 1973, **28,** 512–526.

Bockhoven, J. S. *Moral treatment in American psychiatry.* New York: Springer, 1963.

Bockhoven, J. S. Review of *Concepts of insanity in the United States 1789–1865 by N. Dain. Journal of the History of the Behavioral Sciences,* 1965, **1,** 384–386.

Borkovec, T. D. Autonomic reactivity to sensory stimulation in psychopathic, neurotic, and normal juvenile delinquents. *Journal of Consulting and Clinical Psychology,* 1970, **35,** 217–222.

Bronfenbrenner, U. Reactions to social pressure from adults versus peers among Soviet day school and boarding school pupils in the perspective of an American sample. *Journal of Personality and Social Psychology,* 1970, **15,** 179–189.

Bronfenbrenner, U. *Zwei welten: kinder in USA und UdSSR.* Stuttgart: Deutsche Verlag-Anstalt GmBH, 1972.

Bronfenbrenner, U. Alienation and the American psychologist. *APA Monitor,* 1975, **6,** 9; 10.

Buss, A. H. *Psychopathology.* New York: Wiley, 1966.

Buss, A. R. The emerging field of the sociology of psychological knowledge. *American Psychologist,* 1975, **30,** 988–1002.

Buss, A. R. Development of dialectics and development of humanistic psychology. *Human Development,* 1976, **19,** 248–260.

Butler, C. Hegel and Freud: a comparison. *Philosophy and Phenomenological Research,* 1976, **36,** 506–522.

Campagna, A. F., & Harter, S. Moral judgment in sociopathic and normal children. *Journal of Personality and Social Psychology,* 1975, **31,** 199–205.

Campbell, D. T. On the conflicts between biological and social evolution and between psychological and moral tradition. *American Psychologist,* 1975, **30,** 1103–1126.

Camus, A. *The Stranger* (S. Gilbert, trans.). New York: Knopf, 1960.

Carkhuff, R. R., & Burstein, J. W. Objective therapist and client ratings of therapist-offered facilitative conditions of moderate to low functioning therapists. *Journal of Clinical Psychology*, 1970, **26**, 394–395.

Casper, W., Dahm, I., Giersdorf, P., Rothe, J., & Schuler, H. *Das gesundheitswesen der Deutschen Demokratischen Republik 1975*. Berlin: Nationales Druckhaus Berlin, VOB National AG, 1975.

Cautela, J. R. Covert extinction. *Behavior Therapy*, 1971, **2**, 192–200.

Cauthen, N. Psychopathic personalities and arousal. Paper presented at the meeting of the Midwestern Psychological Association, Cleveland, May, 1972.

Cavior, N., & Dokecki, P. F. The physical attractiveness self concept: A test of Mead's hypothesis. *Proceedings of the 79th Annual Convention of the American Psychological Association*, 1971, 319–320.

Central Bureau of Statistics of Norway. *Mental Hospitals, 1972*. Oslo: Central Bureau of Statistics, 1974.

Christie, R., & Geis, F. *Studies in Machiavellianism*. New York: Academic Press, 1970.

Clausen, J. A. Social patterns, personality, and adolescent drug use. In A. H. Leighton, J. A. Clausen, & R. N. Wilson (Eds.), *Explorations in social psychiatry*. New York: Basic Books, 1957.

Cleckley, H. *The mask of sanity* (3rd ed.). St. Louis: C. V. Mosby, 1955.

Cleckley, H. *The mask of sanity* (4th ed.). St. Louis: C. V. Mosby, 1964.

Cleckley, H. Psychopathic personality. In Ɔ. L. Sills (Ed.), *International encyclopedia of the social sciences* (Vol. 13). New York: Macmillan Co., 1968.

Cleckley, H. *The mask of sanity* (5th ed.). St. Louis: C. V. Mosby, 1976.

Cochrane, R. Crime and personality: Theory and evidence. *Bulletin of the British Psychological Society*, 1974, **27**, 19–22.

Cole, D. L. Teaching the cultural biases of social psychology. Paper presented at the meeting of the American Psychological Association, Washington, D.C., 1976.

Coleman, J. C. *Abnormal psychology and modern life*. (4th ed.). Glenview, Ill.: Scott, Foresman, 1972.

Collins, J. *The existentialists: A critical study*. Chicago: Henry Regnery Co., 1963.

Cooper, B. Psychiatric disorder in hospital and general practice. *Social Psychiatry*, 1966, **1**, 7–10.

Cooper, J. E. The use of a procedure for standardizing psychiatric diagnosis. In E. H. Hare & J. K. Wing (Eds.), *Psychiatric epidemiology*. London: Oxford University Press, 1970.

Corcoran, J. H. Kids, it's Saturday TV again! *The National Observer*, November 8, 1975.

Cvetkovich, G. Dialectic perspectives to empirical research in social psychology. Paper presented at the meeting of the American Psychological Association, Washington, D.C., August 1976.

Davies, J. D. *Phrenology, fad and science*. New Haven: Yale University Press, 1955.

deFundia, T. A., Draguns, J. G., & Phillips, L. Culture and psychiatric symptomatology: A comparison of Argentine and United States patients. *Social Psychiatry*, 1971, **6**, 17–20.

Department of Health and Social Security Office. *Psychiatric Hospitals & Units in England & Wales, 1971*. London, 1973.

Deutsch, M. Theorizing in social psychology. *Personality and Social Psychology Bulletin*, 1976, **2**, 134–141.

Diaz-Guerrero, R. Socio-cultural premises, attitudes and cross-cultural research. *International Journal of Psychology*, 1967, **2**, 79–88.

Dreher, R. H. Origin, development and present status of insanity as a defense to criminal responsibility in the common law. *Journal of the History of the Behavioral Sciences,* 1967, **3,** 47–57.

Duff, A. Psychopathy and moral understanding. *American Philosophical Quarterly,* 1977, **14,** 189–200.

Durkheim, E. Types of suicide. In T. Parsons, E. Shils, K. D. Naegele, & J. R. Pitts (Eds.), *Theories of society* (Vol. 1). New York: The Free Press of Glencoe, 1961. Pp. 213–218.

Eaton, J. W., & Weil, R. J. The mental health of the Hutterites. In A. M. Rose (Ed.), *Mental health and mental disorder.* New York: Norton, 1955.

Elmore, T. M. The development of a scale to measure psychological anomie and its implications for counseling psychology. Paper presented at the meeting of the American Psychological Association, Chicago, September 1965.

Emmons, T. D., & Webb, W. W. Subjective correlates of emotional responsivity and stimulation seeking in psychopaths, normals, and acting-out neurotics. *Journal of Consulting and Clinical Psychology,* 1974, **42,** 620.

Essen-Moeller, E. Individual traits and morbidity in a Swedish rural population. *Acta Psychiatrica et Neurologica Scandanavica,* 1956, Supplement, 100.

Eysenck, H. J. *Crime and personality.* Boston: Houghton-Mifflin, 1964.

Eysenck, H. J. A three-factor theory of reminisence. *British Journal of Psychology,* 1965, **56,** 163–181. (a)

Eysenck, H. J. Biological basis of personality. In G. Lindzey & C. S. Hall (Eds.), *Theories of personality: Primary sources and research.* New York: Wiley & Sons, 1965. (b)

Eysenck, H. J. A brief note on extraversion and performance. *Journal of Abnormal Psychology,* 1974, **83,** 308–310. (a)

Eysenck, H. J. Crime and personality reconsidered. *Bulletin of the British Psychological Society,* 1974, **27,** 23–24. (b)

Eysenck, H. J. Correspondence. *Bulletin of the British Psychological Society,* 1975, **28,** 354–355.

Fortin, R. A. Life, liberty and happiness still an elusive but glittering goal. *The National Observer,* May 29, 1976.

Frankenstein, C. *Psychopathy—a comparative analysis of clinical pictures.* New York: Grune & Stratton, 1959.

Fromm, E. *The sane society.* New York: Rinehart, 1955.

Gale, A. Can EEG studies make a contribution to the experimental investigation of psychopathy? Paper presented at the Advanced Study Institute on Psychopathic Behavior, Les Arcs, Bourg St. Maurice, France, September 1975.

Gergen, K. Social psychology as history. *Journal of Personality and Social Psychology,* 1973, **26,** 309–320.

Gibbins, J. No success please . . . we're British! *Daily Mail,* January 8, 1977.

Glueck, S., & Glueck, E. *Unraveling juvenile delinquency.* New York: The Commonwealth Fund, 1950.

Gnat, T., & Henisz, J. Current developments in social psychiatry in Poland. *Social Psychiatry,* 1966, **1,** 53–56.

Gough, H. G. A sociological theory of psychopathy. *American Journal of Sociology,* 1948, **53,** 359–366.

Guterman, S. S. *The machiavellians.* Lincoln, Nebraska: University of Nebraska Press, 1970.

Guttentag, M. Evaluation and society. *Personality and Social Psychology Bulletin,* 1977, **3,** 31–40.

Guttmacher, M. S. Diagnosis and etiology of psychopathic personalities as perceived in our time. In P. H. Hoch & J. Zubin (Eds.), *Current problems in psychiatric diagnosis.* New York: Grune & Stratton, 1953.

Hacker, D. W. Humanists seek their individual answers—who are we. *The National Observer*, October 18, 1975, p. 22.

Haefner, H. *Psychopathen: daseinanalytische untersuchungen zur struktur and verlaufsgestalt von psychopathien.* Berlin: Springer-Verlag, 1961.

Hammond, K. R., Hursch, C. J., & Todd, F. J. Analyzing the components of clinical inference. *Psychological Review*, 1964, **71**, 438–456.

Hare, R. D. *Psychopathy: theory and research.* New York: Wiley, 1970.

Harrington, A. *Psychopaths.* St. Albans, England: Panther Books, Granada Publishing Limited, 1974.

Hartmann, H. Ego psychology and the problem of adaptation. In D. Rappaport (Ed.), *Organization and pathology of thought.* New York: Columbia University Press, 1951.

Henderson, D. K. *Psychopathic states.* New York: Norton, 1939.

Hendrick, C. Role-taking, role-playing, and the laboratory experiment. *Personality and Social Psychology Bulletin*, 1977, **3**, 467–478.

Hoch, P. H. *Differential diagnosis in clinical psychiatry.* Chicago: Science House, 1972.

Hogan, R. Theoretical egocentrism and the problem of compliance. *American Psychologist*, 1975, **30**, 533–540.

Holland, J. Vergleichende analyse der sowjetischen und amerikanischen psychiatrie. *Medicin in Osteuropa*, 1976, **8**(3), 47–48.

Hollingshead, A. B., & Redlich, F. C. *Social class and mental illness; a community study.* New York: Wiley, 1958.

Hsiau, S. Psychology in China. *American Psychologist*, 1977, **32**, 374–376.

Hughes, J. R., Means, E. D., & Stell, B. S. A controlled study on the behavior disorders associated with the positive spike phenomenon. In N. L. Corah & E. N. Gale (Eds.), *The origins of abnormal behavior.* Reading, Mass.: Addison-Wesley, 1971.

Hunsdahl, J. B. Concerning einfuehling (empathy): A concept analysis of its origin and early development. *Journal of the History of the Behavioral Sciences*, 1967, **3**, 180–191.

Inkeles, A., & Levinson, D. J. National character: the study of modal personality and sociocultural systems. In G. Lindzey & E. Aronson (Eds.), *The handbook of social psychology* (Vol. 4, 2nd ed.). Reading, Mass: Addison-Wesley, 1969.

Institut National de la Sante et de la Recherche Medicale. *Statistiques Medicales des etablissements Psychiatriques.* Année 1971.

Jablensky, A. Personality disorders and their relation to illness and social deviance. *Psychiatric Annuals*, 1976, **6**, 1–12.

Jenkins, R. L. Psychiatric syndromes in children and their relation to family background. *American Journal of Orthopsychiatry*, 1966, **36**, 450–457.

Kallwas, W. *Der psychopath.* Berlin: Springer-Verlag, 1969.

Karpman, B. The myth of the psychopathic personality. *American Journal of Psychiatry*, 1948, **104**, 523–534.

Katchadourian, H. A., & Churchill, C. W. Components in prevalence of mental illness and social class in urban Lebanon. *Social Psychiatry*, 1973, **8**, 145–151.

Katz, R. L. *Empathy, its nature and its uses.* New York: The Free Press, 1963.

Kendell, R. E. The influence of the 1968 glossary on the diagnoses of English psychiatrists. *British Journal of Psychiatry*, 1973, **123**, 527–530.

Koestler, A. *Darkness at noon.* New York: New American Library, 1961.

Kretschmer, E. *Koerperbau und charakter.* Berlin: Springer-Verlag, 1940.

Kuvakin, V. The phenomenon of partiinost: Structure, dynamics, and dialectics: An exposition. *Philosophy and Phenomenological Research*, 1976, **37**, 25–45.

Lange-Eichbaum, W. *Genie, unsinn und ruhm.* Muenchen: Verlag Ernst Reinhardt, 1942.

Leichman, G. A. Is it whether you win or lose, or how you play the game? Paper presented at the British Psychological Society meeting, April 1975.

Levenson, H., & Mahler, I. Attitudes toward others and components of internal–external locus of control. *Psychological Reports*, 1975, **36**, 209–210.

Liebert, R. M., & Schwartzberg, N. S. Effects of mass media. In M. R. Rosenzweig & L. W. Porter (Eds.), *Annual review of psychology,* 1977, **28,** 147–173.

Lindzey, G. Morphology and behavior. In G. Lindzey & C. S. Hall (Eds.), *Theories of personality: Primary sources and research.* New York: Wiley, 1965.

Luchins, A. S. A variational approach to empathy. *Journal of Social Psychology,* 1957, **45,** 11–18.

Luria, A. R. Psychopathological research in the U.S.S.R. In B. Simon (Ed.), *Psychology in the Soviet Union.* Stanford, Calif.: Stanford University Press, 1957.

Lykken, D. T. A study of anxiety in the sociopathic personality. *Journal of Abnormal and Social Psychology,* 1957, **55,** 6–10.

MacCorquodale, K., & Meehl, P. E. On a distinction between hypothetical constructs and intervening variables. *Psychological Review,* 1948, **55,** 95–107.

Maher, B. A. *Principles of psychopathology.* New York: McGraw-Hill, 1966.

Mailer, N. *The white negro.* San Francisco: City Lights Books, 1957.

Marx, K, & Engels, F. *Selected works.* Moscow: Progress Publishers, 1970.

Maslow, A. H. *Toward a psychology of being.* Princeton, N.J.: Van Nostrand, 1962.

McClelland, D. C. *The achieving society.* Princeton, N.J.: Van Nostrand, 1961.

McClelland, D. C., & Winter, D. G. *Motivating economic achievement.* New York: The Free Press, 1969.

McCord, W., & McCord, J. *Psychopathy and delinquency.* New York: Grune & Stratton, 1956.

McCord, W., & McCord, J. *The psychopath: An essay on the criminal mind.* Princeton, N.J.: Van Nostrand, 1964.

McLuhan, M, & Fiore, Q. *The medium is the message.* New York: Bantam, 1967.

McNemar, Q. Lost: Our intelligence? why? *American Psychologist,* 1964, **19,** 871–882.

Mead, G. H. *Mind, self, and society* (C. W. Morris, ed.). Chicago: University of Chicago Press, 1934.

Moore, P. Nader chides researchers, scores testing. *APA Monitor,* November, 1976, 7(11).

Moscovici, S. Society and theory in social psychology. In J. Israel & H. Tajfel (Eds.), *The context of social psychology: A critical assessment.* London: Academic Press, 1972.

Meyers, D. B. Marx and the problem of nihilism. *Philosophy and Phenomenological Research,* 1976, **37,** 193–204.

Mowrer, O. H. What is normal behavior? In A. Wieder (Ed.), *Contributions toward medical psychology.* New York: Ronald Press, 1953.

National Health Service of Denmark. *Medical Report II, Fiscal Year 1969–70.* Copenhagen: National Health Service of Denmark, 1973.

National Institute of Mental Health; Biometry Branch, OPPE. *Trends in resident patients: state and county mental hospitals, 1950–1968.* Chevy Chase, Md.: National Institute of Mental Health, 1970.

Nelson, C. E., & Kannenberg, P. H. Social psychology in crisis: A study of the references in the *Handbook of social psychology* (2nd ed.). *Personality and Social Psychology Bulletin,* 1976, **2,** 14–21.

Nelson, J. G., & Farley, F. H. Creativity and delinquency as a function of arousal and stimulation-seeking: Test of a theory. Paper presented at the meeting of the American Psychological Association, Washington, D.C., August, 1976.

Nixon, R. A. The limitations on the advancement of human welfare under American capitalism. Paper presented at the meeting of the American Psychological Association, Miami, September 1970.

Noel, P. S., & Carlson, E. T. The faculty psychology of Benjamin Rush. *Journal of the History of the Behavioral Sciences,* 1973, **9,** 369–377.

Okanes, M. M. Machiavellian attitudes and choice of values among students in a business college. *Psychological Reports,* 1974, **34,** 1342.

Owen, D. R. The 47, XYY male: A review. *Psychological Bulletin,* 1972, **78,** 209–233.

Page, J. D. Psychopathology: The science of understanding deviance. Chicago: Aldine-Atherton, 1971.

Perkins, S. J. Comment on the news. *United States Armed Forces Radio,* April 22, 1977.

Perry, J. M. Blumenthal's ethic kick. *The National Observer,* January 1, 1977, p. 5.

Petrie, A. *Individuality in pain and suffering.* Chicago: University of Chicago Press, 1967.

Platt, A. M., & Diamond, B. L. The origins and development of the "wild beast" concept of mental illness and its relation to theories of criminal responsibility. *Journal of the History of the Behavioral Sciences,* 1965, **1,** 355–367.

Preu, P. W. The concept of psychopathic personality. In J. McV. Hunt (Ed.), *Personality and the behavior disorders* (Vol. 2), New York: Ronald Press, 1944.

Prociuk, T. J., & Breen, L. J. Machiavellianism and locus of control. *Journal of Social Psychology,* 1976, **98,** 141–142.

Psychiatricka Pece. *Zdsavotnicka Statistika 1972 C.S.S.R.* Rocnik, 1973.

Psychoneurological Institute Department of Health Protection Organization. *Statistical Bulletin Psychiatry 1960–1969.* Warsaw, 1973.

Public Health and Medical Care 1967–1968. *The Official Statistics of Finland XI.* Helsinki, 1970.

Quay, H. C. Psychopathic personality as pathological stimulation seeking. *American Journal of Psychiatry,* 1965, **122,** 180–183.

Quen, J. M. Anglo-American criminal insanity in historical perspective. *Journal of the History of the Behavioral Sciences,* 1974, **10,** 313–323.

Rappaport, J., & Chinsky, J. R. Accurate empathy: Confusion of a construct. *Psychological Bulletin,* 1972, **77,** 400–404.

Raskin, D. C. Psychopathy and detection of deception in a prison population (Report No. 75-1 Contract 75 NI 99-0001). Department of Psychology, University of Utah, June 1975.

Reich, C. A. *The greening of America.* New York: Bantam Books, 1971.

Riegel, K. F. Dialectic operations: The final period of cognitive development. *Human Development,* 1973, **16,** 346–370.

Rogers, C. R. *On becoming a person.* Boston: Houghton-Mifflin, 1961.

Rogers, C. R. *Carl Rogers on encounter groups.* New York: Harper & Row, 1970.

Rollins, N. *Child psychiatry in the Soviet Union.* Cambridge, Mass.: Harvard University Press, 1972.

Rosenthal, D. *Genetic theory and abnormal behavior.* New York: McGraw-Hill, 1970.

Rotenberg, M., & Diamond, B. L. The biblical conception of psychopathy: The law of the stubborn and rebellious son. *Journal of the History of the Behavioral Sciences,* 1971, **7,** 29–38.

Rudin, S. A. National motives predict psychogenic death rates twenty-five years later. In N. L. Corah & E. N. Gale (Eds.), *The Origins of abnormal behavior.* Reading, Mass.: Addison-Wesley, 1971.

Russell, B. *Power: a new social analysis.* London: Allen & Unwin, 1938.

Rychlak, J. F. *A philosophy of science for personality theory.* Boston: Houghton-Mifflin, 1968.

Saenger, G. Psychiatric outpatients in America and The Netherlands: a transcultural comparison. *Social Psychiatry,* 1968, **4,** 149–164.

Saltzstein, H. D. Role-taking as a method of facilitating moral development. Paper presented at the meeting of the Eastern Psychological Association, New York, April 1975.

Sarbin, T. R., Allen, V. L., & Rutherford, E. E. Social reinforcement, socialization, and chronic delinquency. *British Journal of Social and Clinical Psychology*, 1965, **4**, 179–184.

Sartre, J. P. *Being and nothingness: An essay on phenomenological ontology* (H. E. Barnes trans.). New York: Philosophical Library, 1956.

Savino, M. T., & Mills, A. B. The rise and fall of moral treatment in California psychiatry: 1852–1870. *Journal of the History of the Behavioral Sciences*, 1967, **3**, 359–369.

Schachter, S. *Emotion, obesity and crime*. New York: Academic Press, 1971.

Schmauk, F. J. Punishment, arousal, and avoidance learning in sociopaths. *Journal of Abnormal Psychology*, 1970, **76**, 325–335.

Schneider, K. *Die psychopathischen persoenlichkeiten* (4. Auflage). Wien: Deuticke, 1940.

Schneider, K. *Die psychopathischen persoenlichkeiten* (5. Auflage). Wien: Deuticke, 1950.

Scura, W., & Eisenman, R. *Corrective psychiatry and Journal of Social Therapy*, 1971, **17**, 58–64.

Shagass, C., & Overton, D. A. Measurement of cerebral "excitability" characteristics in relation to psychopathology. In M. L. Kietzman, S. Sutton, & J. Zubin (Eds.), *Experimental approaches to psychopathology*. New York: Academic Press, 1975.

Shah, D. K. Sweet-talking ads warp kids' minds, consumerists say. *The National Observer*, December 4, 1976.

Sheldon, W. H. *The varieties of human physique*. New York: Harper, 1940.

Sheldon, W. H. *Varieties of delinquent youth*. New York: Harper, 1949.

Shepard, M. *Fritz*. New York: Dutton, 1975.

Shepherd, M., & Sartorius, N. Personality disorders and the International Classification of Diseases. *Psychological Medicine*, 1974, **4**, 141–146.

Smith, R. J. Some thoughts on psychopathy. *Psychotherapy: Theory, Research, and Practice*, 1973, **10**, 354–358.

Smith, R. J., & Griffith, J. E. Psychopathy, machiavellianism, and anomie. *Psychological Reports*, 1978, **42**, 258.

Snow, D. L., & Newton, P. M. Task, social structure, and social process in the community mental health center movement. *American Psychologist*, 1976, **31**, 582–594.

Solar, S., & Bruehl, D. Machiavellianism and locus of control: Two conceptions of interpersonal power. *Psychological Reports*, 1971, **29**, 1079–1082.

Sontag, L. W. Implications of fetal behavior and environment for adult personalities. *Annals of the New York Academy of Science*, 1966, **134**, 782–786.

Steinberg, E. P., & Schwartz, G. E. Biofeedback and electrodermal self-regulation in psychopathy. *Journal of Abnormal Psychology*, 1976, **85**, 408–415.

Stone, A. A., & Stone, S. S. Confessions of Felix Krull, confidence man (reprinted from T. Mann, *Stories of three decades*, Knopf, 1930). In A. A. Stone & S. S. Stone, *The abnormal personality through literature*. Englewood Cliffs, N.J.: Prentice-Hall, 1966.

Sukhareva, G. E. *Clinical lectures in child psychiatry* (Vol. II). Moscow, 1959.

Sullivan, H. S. *The interpersonal theory of psychiatry*. New York: Norton, 1953.

Syndulko, K., Parker, D. A., Jens, R., Maltzman, I., & Ziskind, E. Psychophysiology of sociopathy: Electrocortical measures. *Biological Psychology*, 1975, **3**, 185–200.

Szasz, T. S. The myth of mental illness. *American Psychologist*, 1960, **15**, 113–118.

Szondi, L. *Triebpathologie, Band I*. Bern: Verlag Hans Huber, 1952.

Tajfel, H., & Moscovici, S. Die wiedergeburt alter Mythen in der socialpsycholgie: ein sonderbares irrlebnis. *Zeitschrift fuer Sozial Psychologie*, 1976, **7**, 292–297.

Tawney, R. H. *Religion and the rise of capitalism*. New York: Mentor Books, 1947.

Taylor, A. J. W. Correspondence. *Bulletin of the British Psychological Society*, 1975, **28**, 285–286.

.The era of limits. *The National Observer*, September, 1976, p. 12.

The visible scientists. *APA Monitor*, 1975, pp. 1; 8.

Tibbetts, P. Pierce and Mead on perceptual immediacy and human action. *Philosophical and Phenomenological Research*, 1975, **36**, 222–232.

Torrance, E. P. *Guiding creative talent*. Englewood Cliffs, N.J.: Prentice-Hall, 1962.

Truax, C. B. Influence of patient statements on judgments of therapist statements during psychotherapy. *Journal of Clinical Psychology*, 1966, **22**, 335–337.

Ullmann, L. P., & Krasner, L. *A psychological approach to abnormal behavior*. Englewood Cliffs, N.J.: Prentice-Hall, 1969.

Van Atta, W. I'll always remember Arthur. *Smith, Kline & French Psychiatric Reporter*, 1965, No. 20, 8–10.

Vaughan, H. G., Jr. Physiological approaches to psychopathology. In M. L. Kietzman, S. Sutton, & J. Zubin (Eds.), *Experimental approaches to psychopathology*. New York: Academic Press, 1975.

Waid, W. M., Orne, M. T., & Wilson, S. K. Sociopathy as a mediating variable in the psychophysiological diagnosis of deception. Paper presented at the meeting of The Society for Psychophysiological research. San Diego, October, 1976.

Wallace, S. R. Achieving research in vivo. (Review of *Motivating economic achievement* by D. C. McClelland & D. G. Winter), *Contemporary Psychology*, 1969, **14**, 635;638;640.

Ward, S., & Wackman, D. B. Children's information processing of television advertising. In P. Clarke (Ed.), *New Models of mass communication (Vol. II)*. Beverly Hills, Calif.: Sage Publications, 1973.

Weber, M. *The Protestant ethic and the spirit of capitalism*. London: Allen & Unwin, 1930.

Weiner, B., & Peter, N. A cognitive-developmental analysis of achievement and moral judgments. *Developmental Psychology*, 1973, **9**, 290–309.

Weinrach, S. G., & Ivey, A. E. Science, psychology and deception. *Bulletin of the British Psychological Society*, 1975, **28**, 263–267.

Wenegrat, A. Linguistic variables of therapist and accurate empathy ratings. *Psychotherapy: Theory, Research and Practice*, 1976, **13**, 30–33.

White, R. W. Competence and the psychosexual stages of development. In M. R. Jones (Ed.), *Nebraska Symposium on Motivation* (Vol. 8). Lincoln: University of Nebraska Press, 1960.

White, R. W. *The abnormal personality*. New York: Ronald Press, 1964.

Whyte, W. H. *The organization man*. New York: Simon & Schuster, 1956.

Wiggins, J. S. Personality structure. In P. R. Farnsworth, M. R. Rosenzweig, & J. T. Palefka (Eds.), *Annual review of psychology*. Palo Alto, Calif.: Annual Reviews, Inc., 1968.

Wolman, B. B. Principles of interactional psychotherapy. *Psychotherapy: Theory, Research and Practice*, 1975, **12**, 149–159.

World Health Organization. *International classification of diseases* (8th Rev.), Geneva, Switzerland: World Health Organization, 1974.

World Health Organization. *Report of the seventh seminar on standardization of psychiatric diagnosis, classification, and statistics*. Tokyo, Japan, 1972.

Zilboorg, G., & Henry, G. W. *A history of medical psychology*. New York: Norton, 1941.

Zubin, J. Classification of the behavior disorders. In P. R. Farnsworth, O. McNemar, & Q. McNemar (Eds.), *Annual review of psychology*. Palo Alto, Calif.: Annual Reviews, Inc., 1967.

Zuckerman, M., Bone, R. N., Neary, R., Mangelsdorff, D., & Brustman, B. What is the sensation seeker? Personality trait and experience correlates of the sensation-seeking scales. *Journal of Consulting and Clinical Psychology*, 1972, **39**, 308–321.

Index

A
B
C   8
D   9
E   0
F   1
G   2
H   3
I   4
J   5